The Politics and Technology of Cyberspace

T0093052

Addressing the problems surrounding cyber security and cyberspace, this book bridges the gap between the technical and political worlds to increase our understanding of this major security concern in our IT-dependent society, and the risks it presents.

Only by establishing a sound technical understanding of what is and is not possible can a properly informed discussion take place, and political visions toward cyberspace accurately map and predict the future of cyber security. Combining research from the technical world that creates cyberspace with that of the political world, which seeks to understand the consequences and uses of cyberspace, Steed analyses and explains the circumstances that have led to current situations whereby IT-dependent societies are vulnerable to, and regularly victims of, hacking, terrorism, espionage, and cyberwar. Two fundamental questions are considered throughout the book: what circumstances led to this state of affairs? And what solutions exist for the future of cyberspace? In tackling these questions, Steed also analyses the emergent and increasingly competing political positions on offer to stabilise the landscape of cyberspace.

This interdisciplinary work will appeal to researchers and students of Security Studies, Intelligence Studies, Strategic Studies and International Relations as well as cybersecurity practitioners charged with developing policy options.

Danny Steed, formerly Lecturer in Strategy and Defence at the University of Exeter, now works at ReSolve Cyber as Head of Strategy, having previously worked for CERT-UK in The Cabinet Office specialising in cyber security. His research interests include strategic theory, strategic history, intelligence, cyber warfare and cybersecurity.

Modern Security Studies
Series editors: Sean S. Costigan and Kenneth W. Estes

This series fills a known gap in modern security studies literature by pursuing a curated, forward-looking editorial approach on looming and evergreen security challenges. Short and long form works will be considered with an eye towards developing content that is widely suitable for instruction and research alike. Works adhere around the series' four main categories: Controversies, Cases, Trends and Primers. We invite proposals that pay particular attention to controversies in international security, notably those that have resulted in newly exposed and poorly defined risks to non-state legitimacy, international or state capacities to act, and shifts in global governance. Case studies should examine recent historical events and security-related actions that have altered present day understanding or political calculations. Trends will need to detail future yet tangible concerns in a 5–10 year timeframe. Authors are also invited to submit proposals to our primers category for short form works on key topics that are referenced and taught throughout security studies.

Verifying Nuclear Disarmament
Thomas Shea

NATO's Democratic Retrenchment
Hegemony after the Return of History
Henrik B. L. Larsen

The Politics and Technology of Cyberspace
Danny Steed

For more information about this series, please visit: www.routledge.com/politics/series/ASHSER1437

The Politics and Technology of Cyberspace

Danny Steed

Routledge
Taylor & Francis Group

LONDON AND NEW YORK

First published 2019
by Routledge
2 Park Square, Milton Park, Abingdon, Oxon OX14 4RN

and by Routledge
605 Third Avenue, New York, NY 10017

First issued in paperback 2021

Routledge is an imprint of the Taylor & Francis Group, an informa business

© 2019 Danny Steed

British Library Cataloguing-in-Publication Data
A catalogue record for this book is available from the British Library

Library of Congress Cataloging-in-Publication Data
A catalog record for this book has been requested

ISBN 13: 978-0-367-78799-8 (pbk)
ISBN 13: 978-1-138-57783-1 (hbk)

Typeset in Times New Roman
by Apex CoVantage, LLC

Contents

Figures

Acknowledgements

All researchers and authors owe a great debt to those who kindly assist them during the trials of piecing together any written work. It is one of the great pleasures of writing to encounter quite so many kind souls who generously donate their time to helping one's own work pass muster. With this in mind I owe my heartfelt thanks to the following people, without whom this work would never have even made it off the drawing board.

Crucially, Dr Simon Anglim who quite simply convinced me to take on a cyber project during this period when I am not presently a full-time scholar. His faith in me being able to take on such a challenge, and his patronage to the editorial team, have been crucial. Next are my editors, Kenneth Estes and Sean Costigan, whose patience and understanding as well as their keen editorial eyes have been much needed throughout. Further to these three are of course the editorial team of the Modern Security Studies Series at Taylor & Francis, who have been no end of help in all the essential mechanics that go into putting a book together once an author has finished with the words.

In addition to the core editorial team are numerous friends and encounters that have all shaped this work for better or worse (the latter being entirely my responsibility of course). In this regard, there are numerous members of Britain's National Cyber Security Centre who have asked to remain anonymous. Their contributions over many snatched lunches, coffees, and correspondences made the world of difference particularly to Chapter 1. Thank you to you technical souls who indulged this charlatan's attempt at Occam's razor in finding the minimalists toolkit!

Thank you too to Emma Rosen, Ilina Georgiva, and Clare Stevens, for your observations throughout writing; to my colleagues at ReSolve Cyber, Jim Wheeler and Jas Mahrra, for their help and patience during my endless ramblings; and to Kathryn Murrell, for her crucial help in constructing original

viii *Acknowledgements*

graphics throughout Chapter 1. For the remaining imagery, thanks must be given to Telegeography for their permission in reproducing their work within. Finally, credit as always to the staff of the RUSI Library, Maughan Library at King's College London, and the British Library for facilitating access to the very necessary streams of resources upon which all researchers need to call.

Introduction

The interconnectedness and openness that the Internet, digital networks, and devices allow have also made securing our cyber landscape a task of unparalleled difficulty. As the world becomes more dependent on the information revolution, the pace of intrusions, disruptions, manipulations, and theft also quickens. Beyond the resulting economic losses and national security threats, our privacy, civil liberties, and constitutional rights – even the voting system that underlies our democracy – all become vulnerable.[1]

Cyber security certainly presents one of the most challenging global security issues society currently faces, further to this it needs to be acknowledged that the concerns range from the incessant stories of cybercrimes and attacks seen on the news, weekly at the very least, but more often than not daily. Anybody with any prior grounding in the history of cyber security and thinking on areas like cyberwar will immediately expect a predictable deluge of views to be cited at this stage. Arquilla and Ronfeldt's 1993 "Cyberwar Is Coming!"[2] very much set the tone for an era of hyperbolic hypothesising that has had an enduring stranglehold on the imagination, even more than two decades later still inspiring similar visions of the commonly referred to "Cyber Pearl Harbor," such as that offered by Richard Clarke, who asks when a nation finds itself paralysed, unable to source food supplies or withdraw cash, 'what will the Commander-in-Chief do?'[3] This kind of thinking has, however, been tempered somewhat by concerted attempts to ground cyber security thinking, most notably by Thomas Rid with his *Cyber War Will Not Take Place* argument.[4]

This seesawing of views on cyber security has not abated, and real-world events have provided much ammunition in forecasting increasing severity of incidents that make the Cyber Pearl Harbor visions not as far-fetched as were previously considered. The occurrences of innovations like the 2009–2010 Stuxnet attack against Iranian nuclear production sites,[5] the

2015–2016 Dyn botnet attack against the Internet of Things,[6] or the 2017 Not-Petya ransomware attack are but three very well-known cases of harm and concern that motivate increasing focus on tackling the challenges of cyber security in the current era. In the case of Not-Petya – to date the case incurring the largest financial impact caused by a single event at more than an estimated $10 billion – the dynamic is clear: 'that it could happen again or even reoccur on a larger scale. Global corporations are simply too interconnected, information security too complex, attack surfaces too broad to protect against state-trained hackers bent on releasing the next world-shaking worm.'[7] Real-world events have led to public warnings such as that issued by the CEO of Britain's nascent National Cyber Security Centre (an offshoot of signals intelligence service GCHQ) Ciaran Martin that a major attack against UK critical infrastructure 'is a matter of when, not if.'[8]

The problem will look no better should one look towards industry for guidance. There, too, readers today will encounter a veritable avalanche of reports and analyses of bewildering data sets and forecasts of criminal activities throughout cyberspace discussing the myriads of ways that harm can be caused. Multiple detailed reports are produced each year, with even a basic Google search returning results including Symantec's *Internet Security Threat Report*,[9] Hewlett Packard's *Cyber Risk Report*[10] or *State of Security Operations*,[11] NTT's *Global Threat Intelligence Report*,[12] or Microsoft's *Security Intelligence Report*,[13] among an array of other lesser-known private bodies. For researchers on cyber security, simply keeping up to speed with the latest industry sources is a daunting prospect. Yes, private bodies such as these are trying to sell their wares, but they are all seeking unique competitive advantage by knowing the current cybercrime trend and, more of value, trying to forecast and mitigate against whatever the next one will be. Simply put, because of the scales of losses incurred by clients globally, there is too big a financial imperative for anybody to get their analyses wrong, and private industry – especially big tech, consultancies, and the financial industry – devote considerable resources to applying analytic method and rigour correctly.

It is into this situation that this work throws its hat, into a history typified by the hyperbolic versus sceptical schools of scholarship, in a world of such incredibly rapid advancement not only in technology, but also in tactical innovation from a bewildering array of actors ranging far beyond the traditional security apparatus of nation states. Yet at its heart, this work seeks to establish that the impact of cyber security runs far deeper than the impact of a particular ransomware strain on the quarterly results of an international corporation, instead trying to frame the fundamental disruption that cyber security has presented to nation states. Specifically, it seeks to chart their struggle not only to come to terms with the insecurities they now face, but also their attempts to reassert sovereign authority into this realm and impose upon it a political vision.

Beyond the incessant and insidious challenges posed by criminals in cyberspace, which are very considerable indeed, it is the political challenges that carry the greatest concern moving ahead in cyberspace. By examining the growing competition between competing political visions – authoritarian versus liberal democratic – a clear geopolitical contest becomes clear with a dominating concern now emerging that the Internet is being leveraged to undermine democracy itself. This is seen first in the broad societal sense, with concerns about the influence of technological addiction and social media platforms among the general populace, a flood of digital information that instead of making us wiser is 'making us more susceptible to nonsense, more emotional, more irrational, and more mobbish.'[14] The patterns of electoral behaviours that have given rise to populist movements motivated by a central, near pathological, *distrust* of established politics[15] are the core proof that this statement from Bartlett bears more truth than not. Throughout the democracies, the political centre grounds have been increasingly abandoned with firm resurgences from the left and right of the political divide. As Adam Piore rightly notes, technology and social media does not cause polarisation like this, 'but it sure helps.'[16]

> We assess that Russian President Vladimir Putin ordered an influence campaign in 2016 aimed at the US presidential election. Russia's goals were to undermine public faith in the democratic process, denigrate Secretary Clinton, and harm her electability and potential presidency. We further assess Putin and the Russian government developed a clear preference for President-elect Trump.[17]

This core finding from the US intelligence community is the heart of the second method of undermining democracy, using *active measures* to apply technology against social divisions for strategic purposes. The findings from US intelligence are nothing short of stunning and have framed (at the time of writing) the continuing investigation by Special Counsel Robert Mueller that will surely be one of the most intriguing reports on American affairs for many years when it does conclude. The problem set at this stage should be abundantly clear – genuine insecurities that plague all users of the Internet have been joined by political desire to shape the future of cyberspace in a manner that suits differing visions of what security itself means. What constitutes security in Washington, DC, is radically different to what it means in Moscow or Beijing. More concerning still to those in the liberal West should be the sobering realisation that now, far from being an inevitable tool of liberation, the Internet has been proven as a potent weapon against democracy itself, the full implications of which are not even at the stage of becoming clear.

The Politics and Technology of Cyber Security seeks to address two fundamental questions, what circumstances led to this state of affairs? And what solutions exist for the future of cyberspace? These questions form the basic structure of the book, with a chapter dedicated to each. To tackle the first question, this author argues that it is certainly necessary for the technological rabbit hole to be explored, as it has been a significant weakness of much analysis to date which has remained ill-informed about the conditioning realities of technology that cyberspace depends on. Only by going beyond the insufficient potted histories of the ARPANET to the World Wide Web can serious assessments be made as to the security implications of the technology upon which our daily lives, economies, and increasingly our critical infrastructure now depend. Once the technology of cyberspace is understood, attention can then turn to matters involving the governance of cyberspace, introducing the intriguing array of bodies and acronyms that comprise the multi-stakeholder approach that is responsible for holding cyberspace together to date. The first chapter will then finish with an extended treatment on the return of politics to cyberspace, outlining the unique historical context that permitted the early growth of the Internet to occur in an apolitical fashion, before dealing with the numerous and increasingly severe run of events and applications by criminals and non-democratic actors that have made the issues of cyber insecurities too big to ignore.

The second chapter focuses on the key political positions that exist for the future of cyberspace, Cyber Sovereignty, and the Free Internet Coalition as it is labelled by Klimburg.[18] These two positions form the geopolitical fault line in cyberspace that will prove the key determinant to its future. Great uncertainty persists about diplomatic progress in cyberspace following the failure of the UN's Group of Government Experts to reach agreement or progress in 2017, with equally strong concern about the seemingly growing appeal among nations of the logic that lies behind Cyber Sovereignty. Most concerning of all, however, is the state of the argument from the Free Internet Coalition, with exploration provided as to what would be needed for the liberal vision to prosper once more. Its core weakness has been that the liberal vision has been taken as a self-evident reality, one that would inevitably spread along with the irresistible tide of technology; this is a view that needs redressing both in theory and most importantly in practice. What this chapter seeks to reveal is not only that there are clear forward positions for the future of cyberspace – and certainly not inevitably liberal ones – but also the fundamental geopolitical importance that its trajectory will have on the development of the multi-polar order in the twenty-first century.

As much as it has attempted to confound traditional strategic and political logic, 'When it comes to geopolitics, cyberspace is clearly an extension of the real world.'[19] Ultimately, although this author is very wary of hyperbolic assertions of looming dystopia, the conclusions to be offered are done so in the spirit of offering a sobering reflection that the Internet of today certainly is not what it was in the 1990s heyday of liberal triumphalism. Further is the realisation that the vision for the Internet – if such a thing ever existed in the first place – as a liberating tool of completely open access to information in the liberal fashion, is now under serious challenge from actors with other visions for world order as the twenty-first century progresses; that vision seeks to convert the Internet 'from a tool of liberation to one of domination.'[20] Those conclusions seek to not only convey the conditioning realities of technology as it continues to develop at ever-increasing rates, but also to place the current and possible futures that cyberspace faces in firmly political terrain. This 'battle for the soul of the Internet'[21] has been raging for years already, with the liberal West either largely ignorant to its occurrence or without a full grasp of its true importance. Whichever path – Cyber Sovereignty or the Free Internet Coalition – gains the most traction and support moving ahead is certain to carry disproportionate effect on the geopolitics of the twenty-first century, for whoever wins will hold the dominating position in shaping the global information flows according to their preferred political designs. This will go far in framing the Internet as one of two things, a tool of freedom or one of control.

Notes

1 Commission on Enhancing National Cybersecurity, *Report on Securing and Growing the Digital Economy* (1 December 2016), p. 3. Available at www. nist.gov/sites/default/files/documents/2016/12/02/cybersecurity-commission-report-final-post.pdf
2 John Arquilla and David Ronfeldt, "Cyberwar Is Coming!" in John Arquilla and David Ronfeldt (eds.), *In Athena's Camp: Preparing for Conflict in the Information Age* (Santa Monica, CA: RAND, 1997).
3 Richard A. Clarke and Robert K. Knake, *Cyber War: The Next Threat to National Security and What to Do About It* (New York: Harper Collins, 2012), p. 260.
4 Thomas Rid, *Cyber War Will Not Take Place* (London: Hurst & Company, 2013).
5 There has been an avalanche of work focused on Stuxnet, but an excellently comprehensive source is Kim Zetter, *Countdown to Zero Day: Stuxnet and the Launch of the World's First Digital Weapon* (New York: Crown Publishers, 2014).
6 A timely report on an incident that the pace of events has left behind already is James Scott and Drew Spaniel, *Rise of the Machines: The Dyn Attack Was Just a Practice Run* (December 2016), Institute for Critical Infrastructure Technology.

Available at https://icitech.org/icit-publication-the-rise-of-the-machines-the-dyn-attack-was-just-a-practice-run/

7 Andy Greenberg, "The Untold Story of NotPetya, the Most Devastating Cyber-attack in History," *Wired* (22 August 2018). Available at www.wired.com/story/notpetya-cyberattack-ukraine-russia-code-crashed-the-world/

8 Ewen MacAskill, "Major Cyber-Attack on UK a Matter of 'when, not if' – Security Chief", *The Guardian* (23 January 2018). Available at www.theguard ian.com/technology/2018/jan/22/cyber-attack-on-uk-matter-of-when-not-if-says-security-chief-ciaran-martin

9 Available at www.symantec.com/security-center/threat-report

10 Available at https://ssl.www8.hp.com/ww/en/secure/pdf/4aa6-3786enw.pdf

11 Available at https://news.hpe.com/state-of-security-operations-2017/

12 Available at www.nttsecurity.com/en-uk/landing-pages/2018-gtir

13 Available at www.microsoft.com/en-gb/security/intelligence-report

14 Jamie Bartlett, *Radicals Chasing Utopia: Inside the Rogue Movements Trying to Change the World* (New York: Nation Books, 2017), p. 9.

15 Roger Eatwell and Matthew Goodwin, *National Populism: The Revolt Against Liberal Democracy* (London: Pelican Books, 2018), p. 23.

16 Adam Piore, "No, Big Tech Didn't Make Us Polarised (but it sure helps)", *MIT Technology Review* (September–October 2018), 121:5.

17 Office of the Director of National Intelligence, *Intelligence Community Assessment: Assessing Russian Activities and Intentions in Recent US Elections* (6 January 2017), p. 2. Available at www.dni.gov/files/documents/ICA_2017_01.pdf

18 Multi-stakeholderism is believed to be too narrow a term to capture the liberal political vision at the heart of the Western counter to Cyber Sovereignty, therefore this author subscribes to Klimburg's more expansive label. Alexander Klimburg, *The Darkening Web: The War for Cyberspace* (New York: Penguin Books, 2017), p. 16.

19 John P. Carlin, *The Code War: America's Battle Against Russia, China, and the Rising Global Cyber Threat* (New York: Public Affairs, 2018), p. 87.

20 Klimburg (2017), p. 316.

21 Nigel Inkster, *China's Cyber Power* (London: IISS, 2016), Ch. 4.

1 What circumstances led to this state of affairs?

1.1 Creating cyberspace: a technology toolkit

A great weakness afflicting the ability of social sciences to debate intelligently the implications of cyber in all its forms – cyber security, cyber warfare, cyber espionage, cyber terrorism and cybercrime, among others – is a lack of affinity with the basic scientific underpinnings and technical realities behind cyberspace itself. Many mistakes indeed have been committed in analyses of the subject, betraying a lack of technological understanding that must be corrected. Doing so need not, however, require exhaustive or even particularly deep dives into realms such as computer science (although anybody truly serious about operating in cyber security would be well-advised to do so); what is needed is an accessible tour of the technical realities that make cyberspace a reality, to provide those from social sciences, the humanities and law with a "toolkit" that allows reasoned assessment as to why those core features, which enabled cyberspace as we now know it to operate, matter in security terms.

There are many representations that seek to articulate the layers composing cyberspace, and NATO's Cooperative Cyber Defence Centre of Excellence (CCDCOE) is quite right to issue its own caveat before any definition: 'There are no common definitions for Cyber terms – they are understood to mean different things by different nations/organisations, despite prevalence in mainstream media and in national and international organisation statement.'[1] This caveat also applies to the layers readers will encounter throughout literature on matters of cyberspace, the British Ministry of Defence (MoD) states its position that cyberspace consists of six interdependent layers: 'social; people; persona; information; network; and real.'[2] The Internet Telecommunications Union (ITU) also offers a high number of layers, listing computers, computer systems, networks and their computer programs, computer data, content data, traffic data, and users.[3] This author chooses to opt for a somewhat more minimalist list, in order to capture the very basic technological essentials that cyberspace requires to operate: the software (logical) level and the physical architecture (geography).[4] While there are of course numerous elements that one can cover, for the purposes of this book it is believed that covering these two areas, with five specific aspects of cyberspace activity, will suffice in outlining both the technical operation and their necessary security aspects concerning cyber security.

The software layer

Packet switching

There is little need to try and provide any sort of generic history of the Internet as a whole, this has been mightily achieved from those working on the technical side of cyberspace affairs,[5] in social science,[6] and in general history.[7] The focus here instead is on outlining the key elements of cyberspace, beginning with packet switching. Packet switching is the core element that differentiates[8] cyberspace and the Internet from previous means of transmitting information; the immediate predecessor services – the telephone and the telegraph networks – relied on circuit switching. Very simply, circuit switching was a linear, manual connection that had to be maintained for any single call or point of transmission to be successfully made – 'a set of switches creates a dedicated circuit for signals to go back and forth';[9] were any flaw or failure in the circuit to occur, the transmission would be lost. Not only this, but the entirety of the data needed to flow through that single circuit, leaving it very vulnerable to intercept as a key security concern.

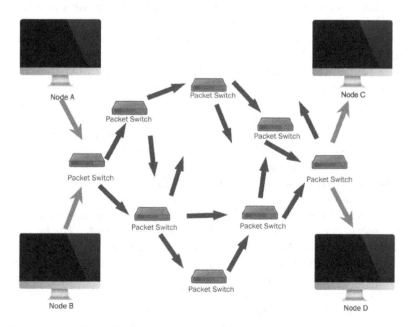

Figure 1.1 Packet switching

A question becomes apparent right from the start, why was packet switching needed at all? The problem set that faced some of the earliest forerunners of cyberspace, in particular those establishing the ARPANET, is best outlined by Isaacson:

> Would communication between two places on the network require a dedicated line between them, as a phone call did? Or was there some practical way to allow *multiple* data streams to share lines simultaneously, sort of like a time-sharing system for phone lines?[10]

The solution was packet switching:

> a special type of store-and-forward switching in which the messages are broken into bite-size units of the exit same size, called packets, which are given address headers describing where they should go. These packets are then sent hopping through the network to their destination by being passed along from node to node, using whatever links are most available at that instant.[11]

A key aspect to note that is not immediately obvious in Isaacson's articulation is the fact that those packets are 'separately transmitted along different routes and then reassembled when they arrive at their destination.'[12] As the Internet Society rightly states, the innovation of packet switching was the key element in allowing a core technical principle of what later become known as the Internet to emerge – open architecture networking. This open architecture was made possible by packet switching; without it, the only reliable way of federating networks was to rely on circuit switching.[13]

The innovation of packet switching raises the necessary question for readers of this work, why does this matter in security terms? First is the recognition that packet switching offers the internetting[14] concept a greater degree of resilience than circuit switching could ever provide, which harks back to the classic, simplistic idea that the Internet was built to survive a nuclear war.[15] When all works as intended, the packet finds the most efficient route to its destination computer, but should any disruption or blockage occur, the packet simply 'consults a routine table to determine the next best step and to send the packet closer to its destination.'[16] The ability for a data packet to reroute time and again throughout the network, even when encountering blocked, denied, or disrupted nodes, effectively circumvents the primary weakness pervasive in the circuit switching model, and provides a network ability to survive the disruption or even destruction of portions of its nodes. Interception or denial of communications becomes a much harder proposition to achieve with such technology, as it is much harder to know what routes are being taken or even how to effectively deny service in a targeted fashion.

Secondly, the sheer resilience of cyberspace networks poses a security challenge to the state itself, one that Dunn Cavelty and Brunner have already stated, that increasing internationalisation and privatisation have been enhanced by these technological developments, diminishing the importance of the state.[17] That diminishment lies in the reduction of the state's monopoly over information itself, enabling the creation of new breeds of non-state actors to operate in this low cost of entree space. Actors such as WikiLeaks, Anonymous, and the range of advanced persistent threat (APT) groups are the clearest example of those widely known about, who have delivered disproportionate effect through their actions in cyberspace. If a state wishes to throttle and block the dissemination of information, packet switching is a reliable and automated means of ensuring that the packets simply find the most reliable route – through, around, and beyond sovereign territorial boundaries – to its recipient. If 'Information is a key way by which . . . power operates and develops,'[18] then packet switching is a key enabler for the distribution of information, and therefore power, away from the state and to the individual.

TCP/IP

If packet switching enabled the ability to send data across and between potentially unlimited numbers of networks, the next question to be raised was, by which standard would computers, networks, and packets communicate with each other? This problem set is well articulated by Tarnoff, in that 'getting networks to talk to one another – internetworking – posed a whole new series of difficulties, because the networks spoke alien and incompatible dialects.'[19] Data simply could not be exchanged and read without a universal common language for understanding on all sides. The requirement, then, was to build a standard language by which all networks could operate, ensuring that networks worldwide could seamlessly accept and exchange the packets being sent. Without a shared protocol language, the needs of an open architecture network environment could not be met, but the protocol that solved the problem would come to be called the Transmission Control Protocol/Internet Protocol (TCP/IP).

TCP/IP 'provided all the transport and forwarding services in the Internet.'[20] Several versions were, as expected, necessary in order to provide the required level of reliability in global interchanging, making use of the underlying network service of cyberspace, in order to cope with the prospect of missing or lost data packets. TCP is the top layer of the protocol, which is responsible for accepting large segments of data and breaking it down into packets for sending; IP is the bottom layer, responsible for the locational aspects of sending data, allowing packets to get to the correct destination.[21]

TCP/IP requires four layers to operate and are the foundation on which data exchange at the software level occurs in cyberspace. These layers are named the DARPA model (shown in Figure 1.2): the Application Layer, the Host-to-Host Transport Layer, the Internet Layer, and the Network Interface Layer. Applications access the services of the other three layers through the Application Layer, which determines the protocols needed to exchange information for whichever application is being used. The Transport Layer enables the connection to the Internet Layer, readying the TCP protocol for data exchange according to the specified protocol identified at the Application Layer. The Internet Layer brings IP into operation, deploying the addressing, packaging, and routing functions. Finally, the Network Interface Layer places data packets on the network medium and ensures connection between different network models.[22]

This apparently humble ability – to split data into packets and send/retrieve those packets to/from the correct destination across differing network types – enabled a huge leap in the capacity of cyberspace; TCP/IP had provided a general purpose service, a general infrastructure that could operate globally, enabling waves of applications that had not yet been conceived.[23] The ARPANET transitioned to TCP/IP in its entirety on 1 January 1983, following its adoption as the defence standard earlier in 1980.[24]

How TCP / ICP works

Step 1:
Data is broken
into packets
by the TCP protocol

Step 2:
The IP protocol moves
the packets over the
internet

Step 3:
Data is
reassembled into
a whole by the
TCP protocol

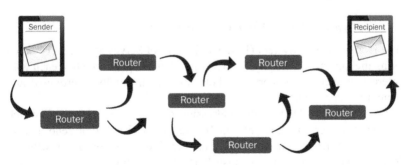

Figure 1.2 TCP/IP

This adoption became key for what is today a common industry term – scaling. Blum is perfectly succinct in showing how the TCP/IP adoption resulted in an accelerating growth of connected networks and computers around the world:

- 1982: 15 connected networks
- 1986: more than 400
- 2011: more than 35,000
- 1985: 2,000 computers with Internet access
- 1987: 159,000
- 2011: 2,000,000,000[25]

As above with packet switching, the question remains as to what the security implications are of the ability to connect all computers and networks globally. The argument here is that this lies in two places; first, the ability to connect all networks and computers globally results in the potential ability to access all connected information.[26] Second, by creating a globally accessible, common environment that has grown to the level of a societal dependency (indeed even a human right), a whole new attack surface has been created – one with arguably the lowest cost of entry of all time – enabling not only legitimate transfer of data and services, but also of cyber espionage, cybercrime, and cyber warfare. With so much to gain from being connected on a legitimate level, there is equally as much to gain from exploiting cyberspace for illegal and malicious purposes. Global connectivity, available 24/7, means an attack surface open to as many people as are connected, creating the challenge of understanding even what the risks are, posed by whom, at what scale, originating from where, acting to what purpose, and with what effect. These are some of the most potent security concerns that result as part of the information revolution brought forward, with cyberspace enabling just about any and all security actors to operate within.

Domain Name System (DNS) and Root Server System

The Domain Name System (DNS) and the Root Server System very much bring the logical and the physical realities of cyberspace together, each with interesting security concerns, as both are fundamentally intertwined and cannot be separated.

In essence, the DNS is the addressing system of the Internet,[27] which translates a user's request into an IP address to visit and/or send/receive data to/from. DNS is also sometimes referred to *as* the root zone, with the Root Server System acting as a distributed network of physical servers upon which to process and direct those address requests from users as they come

Root level

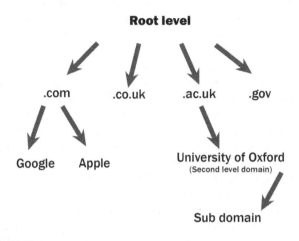

.com   .co.uk   .ac.uk   .gov

Google   Apple   **University of Oxford**
                            (Second level domain)

                                            Sub domain

Figure 1.3 DNS

in. The Root Server System is the top-level layer of the DNS hierarchy providing IP addresses for users,[28] and just below this top-level layer lies the domain level itself, where operators make provision for domain registrations like. com or. org etc.[29] ICANN best explains the user journey at this point:

> So instead of typing 207.151.159.3, you can type www.internic.net. It is a mnemonic device that makes addresses easier to remember. The DNS translates the domain name you type into the corresponding IP address, and connects you to your desired website. The DNS also enables email to function properly, so the email you send reaches the intended recipient.[30]

Baranowski helps to complete the explanation in saying that the root name server provides the phone number in the form of an IP address, while the domain name that a user inputs – Google, for example – is the phone book name. The top-level DNS handles the translation between the domain name and the generic IP address, with each root name server maintaining the list of registered domains with which to correspond IP addresses.[31]

Cyberspace cannot function without its logical layer processes or submarine cable for signals to traverse; the DNS and Root Server System is also crucial to the operation of the Internet as we know it. As without TCP/IP packets could not be created to send, without submarine cables there would be no infrastructure to send them across, and without DNS there would be no way for users to know where to send their packets. Without the Root Server System, there would be no distributed network of servers across the world to process the requests for packets. The systems at this point are so symbiotic that they need to be referred to in unison, as their operation is a crucial top layer to the network. 'Close coordination of root zone updates and continuous surveillance of the servers by the root server operators contribute to the stable operation of the Internet.'[32] Cerf's statement here speaks to the central importance of the root zone and DNS; they are the linchpin of stability in the system, ensuring the smooth flow of traffic from all requests.

Why does the DNS and Root Server System matter in security terms? First is for DNS; as the entire system is built on trust, DNS is ultimately both vulnerable to and at the same time necessary for the processing of attacks on other areas of cyberspace. The system works exceptionally well when trust is adhered to by users, 'but it can be broken, either by accident or by maliciously feeding the system bad data.'[33] Feeding bad data essentially means spoofing the DNS to launch attacks (or simply redirect traffic from its true location to an assailant's own desired area[34]), which is a favoured vector in cyber attacks, regardless of the nature of the attack used, be it DDoS (TCP SYNN flood attacks), payload intrusion (cache poisoning attacks), traffic redistribution (man-in-the-middle attacks) or phishing and social engineering in its many forms.[35] So vital is DNS to the ubiquity of cyber attacks that the nascent National Cyber Security Centre (NCSC) in Britain has centred its flagship defence program – Active Cyber Defence – on DNS filtering in order to reduce the attack footprint in the UK. This program has completed its first year of live operations in 2017 with significant collaboration between that organisation and the UK domain providers – Nominet and British Telecom (BT) – to scale DNS filtering first to the Public Service Network in order to provide proof of concept for wider application across UK cyberspace.[36] Rosenzweig is wrong in his argument that if DNS were to be corrupted or hijacked communications across the Internet would break down;[37] the brutal fact is that DNS is corrupted and hijacked constantly as a facilitator of attacks, hence DNS was central to the NCSC's early efforts in Britain.

Second is the Root Server System, which presents an interesting bottleneck that has given rise to a near myth in cyberspace; that of there being just 13 root servers propping up the whole Internet. There are indeed 13 root servers that underpin the Internet, but the term is used to indicate IP root *zones*, not merely physical servers. This very small number exists due to the limitations of an essential packet type that precedes a TCP conversion to be sendable across the Internet – UDP. A UDP packet is a maximum of 512 bytes, which can only house a maximum of 13 network addresses to send it to. Thirteen was therefore agreed upon as the most secure and efficient way to underpin the network without compromising the operation of either UDP or TCP packets before they have even been created.[38] The myth should be corrected, however, even though it is grounded more in misunderstanding than anything else. There are indeed 13 root server zones, but these are represented by 'many hundreds of root servers at over 130 physical locations in many different countries.'[39]

The security implication, however, is easy to misread at this point. The implication is that, even with large volumes of physical site redundancy, at the logical level the Root Server System is capable of being attacked due to its very small zonal configuration. The Root Server System has been the subject of outages due to technical glitches twice – 1997 and 2000[40] – and to at least three large scale attacks – 2002,[41] 2007,[42] and 2016[43] – intended to disrupt or take down the entire Internet; indeed these attacks have prompted the greater physical distribution of servers in order to reduce the effectiveness of similar future attacks. But these incidents have shown that, despite the efforts at increased distribution globally, the underlying root system of the Internet can indeed be attacked.

Physical architecture

Submarine cables

The solutions created at the logical level – that fundamentally enabled the creation of this virtual world – begs another question as to how cyberspace works, where do the connections occur? The answer reveals an unpalatable reality; that cyberspace not only has, but also is fundamentally dependent upon, a physical geographically based architecture. Nowhere is this more real than in the critical role played by submarine cables.

Submarine cables matter most above other physical components of transmission (notably, orbital satellites) for one reason: the very vast bulk of all content traversing cyberspace does so through submarine cables. Estimates can vary on the exact amount, with the International Cable Protection Committee (ICPC) stating it to be over 95%,[44] the UK Policy Exchanges holds the figure at 97%,[45] whereas Parag Khanna goes even further, stating that submarine cables 'crisscross the earth like yarn wrapped around a ball, carrying 99 percent of intercontinental data traffic.'[46] Single cables within that yarn carry as much as 160 terabits of data across the Atlantic *every second*.[47] This matters so intently simply because of the naive impressions that seem to exist regarding cyberspace and the Internet more generally, as Blum sagely puts it, 'The preferred image of the Internet is instead a sort of nebulous electronic solar system, a cosmic "cloud." '[48] Reality could not be further from the truth; cyberspace is not a purely virtual space at all, totally

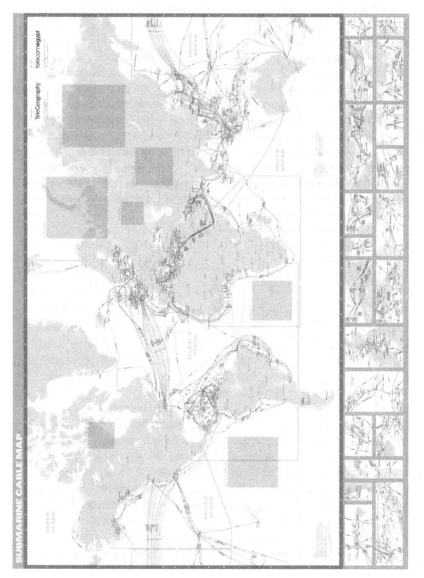

Figure 1.4 Submarine cable map

devoid of geography and indeed "up in the cloud." There is a physical reality to cyberspace that is made nowhere more pronounced than via submarine cables, the "tubes" through which cyberspace exists.[49]

Geography is not dead, nor has distance died[50] because of cyberspace, and – while the author indeed concedes that relative speed is hugely condensed in cyberspace, with actors able to interact globally at the speed of light without physical proximity to one another – because those deaths are not only premature, but also indeed ultimately nonsensical ones, geography does indeed still matter a very great deal with regards to cyber security. Before engaging those concerns, however, it is necessary to capture how the submarine cables work, even though this is ultimately far simpler than recounting the previous logical level innovations.

Simply put, once the TCP/IP protocols split a user's data into packets and identify the correct IP address to send them to, the transmission then becomes an electronic signal, a light beam that is sent via cables. The user journey begins on their own device, which (even if starting from a wireless connection) will connect to your network cable (whether at the home, workplace, or elsewhere), which will then connect to the regional trunk cable or junction. At this point the signals will transit submarine cables towards the destination IP address, entering another national territory and traverse the local cable exchanges before packets are reassembled at the destination. This all of course happens at just about the speed of light, with packets perhaps using several different submarine cables to find their route, crossing multiple nations en route.

A real-world example will serve at this point to draw out the significance. To pick one of the busiest, most frequently accessed services on the Internet – Facebook – if a user in the UK wants to access and use data from that site, their request must be served by the Node Pole data centre that Facebook maintains in Lulea, north Sweden.[51] European requests for Facebook services ultimately are responded to by this data centre, with submarine cables carrying the millions upon millions of requests to and from their destination. As Blum says, 'In basest terms, the Internet is made of pulses of light.'[52] The vast majority of those pulses of light travel through submarine cables that are very much grounded in physically real geography, bringing with it the reality that cyberspace itself can be impacted by the physically real world.

Why should this matter in security terms? In the first, and worst, instance, these cables can be attacked by actors seeking to disrupt the activities of an opponent. Simply put, as a nation becomes more connected to and dependent upon cyberspace, that nation's relative vulnerability to cyber attack increases in kind.[53] Furthermore, being able to disrupt the primary use of connected infrastructure through denial of access to submarine cables could have catastrophic impact upon a nation's ability to communicate, trade, and conduct financial transactions, among numerous other applications.

Sunak's 2017 *Policy Exchange* paper on the insecurity of submarine cables illustrates these impacts very well, noting the case where damage caused by civilian ships to submarine cables between Italy and Egypt in December 2008 reduced traffic between Europe and the Middle East by 80%. This impacted American military forces in Iraq at the time, who had to reduce their daily unmanned aerial vehicle (UAV) sorties from Balad Air Force Base from the hundreds to the tens due to a lack of available bandwidth.[54] The ability to attack submarine cables – of which there are only an estimated 213 systems worldwide[55] – can have disproportionate impact on a society's economy, and must surely be considered a prime strategic option in an area where more than $10 trillion is transmitted *daily*.[56]

The second reason why submarine cables matter in strategic terms is that, when one considers that there are only 213 networks worldwide, bottlenecks in traffic throughout cyberspace are by definition created. If bottlenecks bring the vast bulk of traffic through certain national geographies, this presents a highly valuable intelligence opportunity to any security actor willing to exploit it. Readers need look only to the Edward Snowden revelations for how this has already been achieved by the American National Security Agency (NSA) and Britain's Government Communications Headquarters (GCHQ). Of the many secrets that Snowden betrayed, critical to Anglo-American intelligence gathering efforts was a program code-named Tempora,[57] which was a British collection method based on the interception of Internet communications from submarine cables landing in American or British sovereign territory, with retrospective analysis of data for up for 30 days following collection.[58] The success of Anglo-American efforts are beyond the mandate of this discussion; suffice to say for the moment, however, that simply the fact that an intelligence service has already mastered a technique for intercepting communications via submarine cables reveals that cyberspace, and the tubes through which more than 95% of all global data and communications traverse, makes those cables the number one intelligence target in the world. *The Guardian* was not wrong to label GCHQ an 'intelligence superpower' for its achievement;[59] whoever can master, control, and exploit the submarine cables to best effect will develop a very valuable geopolitical advantage.

Data centres

The final segment of the physical layer addresses a fundamental point, where does data sleep?[60] The answer, much akin to the role of submarine cables, is so simple as to almost be banal; data is housed in data centres scattered worldwide.

Earlier, when recounting the fundamentals of how a user accessed information, Facebook's data centre in Sweden was used as an example of how

Figure 1.5 Data centre map

European users connect to the service. The data centre is simply the destination for user requests on a particular service, in Facebook's case, storing
user photos, posts and such, and pushing out the feed to users' devices.
Even the notion of the "cloud," where you or your workplace's data is not
physically stored onsite but on the cloud, also means only that the data is
physically housed elsewhere. Blum is right in stating that the data centre is
the closest thing 'the Internet has to a physical vault.'[61]

A vault is indeed a prescient description from Blum, for how data centres
work is ultimately an extremely simple matter; it is instead the security
consequences they present that are of far greater concern here. In the first
instance is trust; your data is trusted to a third-party organisation to store,
process, transmit and keep safe from all those who should not be able to
access it. This now even applies to intelligence services, with the Amazon
Web Services now openly advertising its Secret Region service, specifically designed to provide cloud solutions of information up to Top Secret
level.[62] Indeed, this Secret Region is the result of a $600 billion contract that
Amazon won from the Central Intelligence Agency in 2013 to cater specifically to Top Secret cloud storage requirements.[63] In a post-Snowden world,
whom you trust your data to is an extremely sensitive affair, most especially
for intelligence services, who have suffered unprecedented data breaches
in the past decade, providing precious insights into their inner workings.
Where you store your data is critical to knowing where your own assets are,
it is also important as, should anybody be able to gain knowledge of exactly
which centres you use and where they are, they then have a target to breach
in search of your data. When it comes to where you choose to store your
data, trust is the first security concern at play.

The second security concern brings home the physical reality of cyberspace once more: a physical storage location is open to physical damage.
Some may argue that the notion of physically attacking data is nonsense, but
there is an intriguing case study to reveal how this can be done, even if by
complete accident. On the morning of Sunday, 6 December 2005, just north
of London at Hemel Hempstead, the largest explosion in Europe since the
Second World War happened at the Buncefield oil depot, measuring 2.3 on
the Richter scale.[64] A little-known fact about Buncefield was not the depot
itself, but that the headquarters – and data centre – for Northgate Information Solutions was the next closest business to the depot. Northgate suffered
significant physical damage to its data centre, in which some 90% of all UK
local government authorities housed their data,[65] with almost total impact
on every system housed: '212 systems relating to 209 customers needed
to be re-established.'[66] These were implemented in a disaster recover protocol at an alternative site using backup tapes that were at this point just
over 24 hours old,[67] yet the impact was still severe for many, with Haringey

Council in London being unable to process online council tax payments for over a month after the explosion.[68] Likewise, several hospitals in the UK used the site for data storage and were significantly impacted; Addenbrookes hospital – based in Cambridge – was forced to revert to a paper system to process data, as its entire server system was based at Northgate's Hemel Hempstead location, as were the systems of two other NHS Trusts across the country.[69] The Buncefield oil disaster vividly demonstrates the fragility of data centres to a physical event, having significantly affected local governance and healthcare in the UK; even if one only achieves a 24-hour effect on the data operations of major security actors like military units or intelligence services, it is immediately apparent how serious such disruption could be.

This concludes the minimalist's toolkit for understanding the technology underpinning cyberspace, which serves to condition the fundamental security aspects presented by its use. It has been shown that cyberspace most certainly is not beyond physical geography and does not render its influence incomplete. Both where data is stored and the journey it must take throughout cyberspace carries significant physical dependencies that have been exploited and compromised in the pursuit of security objectives. And on the logical level, particularly through the DNS system, it is a system reliant on trust; this very much frames the persistent problem of attribution encountered in reality, for it is the vulnerability in DNS systems that has been shown to be exploited in vast volumes by those carrying out attacks like large-volume phishing campaigns. Ultimately, although the Internet was always designed with high levels of resiliency in mind, it also contains fundamental insecurities that present persistent security concerns worldwide.

1.2 Internet governance

Armed with the knowledge of how cyberspace operates, it is now necessary to explore and understand how cyberspace has been governed to date. Internet governance is, unsurprisingly, an exceedingly complex proposition, for an equally simple reason: 'Nobody owns the Internet.'[70] The innovations revealed previously, those that enabled an explosion in the growth of cyberspace that dwarfs even that of the Industrial Revolution, have consequently built a system – thousands upon thousands upon thousands of interconnected networks – that is constructed, owned, used, and relied on by a vast number of different stakeholders. Due to this complexity, a difficult fact must be accepted, that the Internet 'has no single governing body.'[71] The task here, therefore, is to examine what Internet governance is and how it has been achieved within a system that is inherently built and enabled by empowering the widest possible number of participants .

What is Internet governance? Governance can encompass a multitude of aspects, 'a wide field including infrastructure, standardisation, legal, socio-cultural, economic and development issues.'[72] But at its core, 'to talk about internet governance is to talk about the complex system of relationships and regulations that allow all those computers to communicate.'[73] More officially, in 2005 the UN-sponsored World Summit on the Information Society issued the accepted definition as:

> The development and application by governments, the private sector and civil society, in their respective roles, of shared principles, norms, rules, decision-making procedures, and programs that shape the evolution and use of the Internet.[74]

This definition frames the governance concept entirely as a multi-stakeholder one, whereby no singular authority can rule supreme. Klimburg is quite right to note accordingly that the Internet is not only a technical but also a policy and governance marvel, due to its success in successfully governing such a complex galaxy of stakeholders for so long.[75] This multi-stakeholder model is dependent on the trust and willingness to cooperate among the stakeholders; 'it cannot and will not function without the cooperation and collaboration of the entire range of entities with interest in its operation.'[76] This, however, creates a logical mess, a veritable 'miniature galaxy of individuals and organisations . . . often coexisting rather than cooperating'[77] in the pursuit of keeping cyberspace open and accommodating to all.

Clearly then, the answer to the question of who governs the Internet is going to be a messy one. In this, Klimburg is right to remind readers that we must accept governance as roughly split into two components: technical and policy governance.[78] The first place to begin is on that technical front with the Internet Engineering Task Force (IETF), which 'develops new Internet standards and protocols and modifies existing ones for better performance.'[79] Yannakogeorgos describes the IETF in even simpler terms in his article, in describing the organisation as the 'Stewards of TCP/IP,'[80] the essential protocol on which global Internet traffic is based that was explored earlier. The IETF meets three times a year and makes decisions on the most important protocols to the Internet's operation, such as DNS, through membership that is effectively open to all, with decision-making based on achieving consensus.[81]

Despite the obvious importance of the IETF to governance in keeping those global standards current, however, Klimburg is right to emphasise a point that begins to reveal the inherent complexity in governance structures. Very simply the IETF does not exist as a legal entity; 'legally speaking, it is a subchapter of another organisation, the non-profit Internet Society (ISOC).'[82] The Internet Society was formed in 1992, and 'came about when Internet Governance moved beyond just matters of technical coordination.'[83] As the Internet went global, many participants worried about the centrality – and thereby dominance – of US government involvement, and the ISOC was created in order to begin addressing the disputes surrounding governance decisions. ISOC declares their mission accordingly:

> The Internet Society supports and promotes the development of the Internet as a global technical infrastructure, a resource to enrich people's lives, and a force for good in society. Our work aligns with our goals for the Internet to be open, globally-connected, secure and trustworthy. We seek collaboration with all who share these goals.[84]

Membership is open to all, with members electing trustees to the Internet Advisory Board (IAB), who oversee these governance processes on behalf of the community of members. As an independent, international organisation, ISOC helped to create an interesting fork in the road, one that sought to keep policy as separate from technical matters as possible. Klimburg reveals the nub of his critical point at this stage, when he rightly draws out the desire of the IETF to operate as a purely technical function, avoiding the political; 'which is why the IETF functions the way it does: keeping policy and politics as far away from itself as possible.'[85]

The next organisation to consider is of course the best known among the alphabet soup of players, the Internet Corporation for Assigned Names and Numbers (ICANN). If technical matters are decided in places like the IETF, and ownership of actual infrastructure is a matter for the private sector, then ICANN has become the battleground for the public disputes over network policy.[86] The need for a new body chimed perfectly with the needs of the 1990s; the global Internet was exploding in users following the rollout of the World Wide Web – supported by legislation such as the 1992 High Performance Computing and Communications Act (commonly known as the Gore Bill)[87] – it was only logical that such an explosion in ordinary, non-technical users would precipitate governance challenges that went beyond the technical. ICANN has since become a focal point for these concerns.

ICANN was established in 1998 through a contract with the US Department of Commerce, with the declared mission to 'coordinate, at the overall level, the Internet's system of unique identifiers, and in particular to ensure the stable and secure operation of the Internet's unique identifier systems.'[88] This coordination is for three things: protocol assignments (through IETF); Internet number resources (IP addresses); and root zone management (the DNS system).[89] It does these through the coordination of the Internet Assigned Numbers Authority (IANA) functions, which are listed as:

> (1) the coordination of the assignment of technical protocol parameters including the management of the address and routing parameter area (ARPA) top-level domain; (2) the administration of certain responsibilities associated with Internet DNS root zone management such as generic (gTLD) and country code (ccTLD) Top-Level Domains; (3) the allocation of Internet numbering resources; and (4) other services.[90]

ICANN operates a governance structure that includes a board of directors, but relies fundamentally on a bottom up multi-stakeholder model that is consensus driven; '. . . ultimate decision making resides largely within the board, with fifteen directors (plus four non-voting liaisons), which also appoints the chief executive officer. This board is also the result of a bottom-up process by which prospective members are nominated from a host of various organisations . . .'[91] The spirit of this model is that 'All points of view receive consideration on their own merits. ICANN's fundamental belief is that all users of the Internet deserve a say in how it is run.'[92] Alongside the Internet, ICANN too has grown significantly during its 20 years of operating, 'from a marginal budget of less than $1 million in 1999 to $60 million in 2010 and around $160 million in 2015.'[93]

ICANN is not a perfect organisation however, nor are its operation viewed as entirely objective and benevolent, instead 'many still see ICANN as captive to US interests.'[94] Such a view persists even after the US Government's formal relinquishing of its contractual oversight of ICANN, announced in 2014 and finalised in 2016. Lucas puts the reason why in blunter terms, when he says that 'ICANN has few friends. It is seen as secretive, dominated by Western, male engineering types, and prone to security lapses.'[95] Most significantly, however, is the suspicion among nations of the lack of government representation in this governance model, with Klimburg citing Vladimir Putin's infamous declaration that the entire Internet project was little more than a 'CIA project,'[96] as indication of how deeply ingrained is the belief of Western bias in the governance model.

Critiques such as the above however, are in many respects misplaced and indeed also obfuscate a key reason why the American Federal Government established ICANN to begin with. With the explosive growth of the Internet, and the need for some kind of dedicated governance, the Clinton Administration recognised the early political challenges from other states – notably Russia and China – who believed in a multilateral approach to governance. This was to be achieved by subsuming Internet governance under the mandate of the existing International Telecommunications Union (ITU), a UN body that was ultimately subject to state control via the UN.[97] The criticisms of ICANN being a puppet of American interests deliberately ignore the context of its creation in the first place, which was precisely to avoid placing the Internet under state control. And, as Raustiala rightly establishes, the relinquishment of formal American government involvement in 2016 by the Obama Administration was a decision intended to 'protect the fundamental features of the Internet nearly everyone cares about most: its openness, diversity, and fundamental resilience.'[98]

It is necessary at this stage to issue some key characteristics of the current governance system in place. Four defining characteristics are proposed that make up the key tenets of Internet governance at this point: first, it emerged from technical, not political, necessity; secondly, the nature of the venture produced a multi-stakeholder model; thirdly and consequently, an apolitical model was born; and finally, that these components together have laid the seeds of political challenge to change this status quo as the expansion of cyberspace and the Internet has matured alongside its inevitable security concerns.

Governance is a technical, not a political, necessity

Notwithstanding the elements of truth behind the Internet's origin as an ARPA-funded research project – already dealt with in section 1.1 above, but it is important again to note Isaacson's contribution to tempering the mythology surrounding this origin,[99] as well as fully accept ARPA's role[100] – the creation of cyberspace was above all else a research-driven technical achievement. That quantum leap in technology did, for a time, not need a wide-ranging governance model simply because its global penetration had not yet scaled in the manner to necessitate one. This of course began to change with the roll out of TCP/IP in 1983 that made a global Internet a reality, but forever changed later with the World Wide Web (coinciding with the increasing availability of the Personal Computer),[101] which opened the gates to the Internet for all and ignited an explosion in users that is simply staggering in its scale.

Even then, however, the need for governance was driven not by any political agenda or requirement, but simply in the technical ability to cope with the increased demand on the networks. The need was to distribute domain names, not political messages; to issue IP addresses, not register voters; and to scale the technological infrastructure – data centres, cabling, and submarine cables – to match user demand and the migration of the global economy from analogue to digital. Cyberspace, like all spaces, needed to be governed less it fell apart before reaching its true potential, yet its governance was necessitated by the technical need to operate what is above all a technical space, not a political need or desire to do so. Indeed the limits of political interest can effectively be labelled as actions to enable and catalyse the explosive growth that transpired in the 1990s, through legislation to support the roll out like the aforementioned "Gore Bill" of 1992, among other lesser known acts. Intriguingly, therefore, Internet governance may arguably be historically unique in establishing itself as a primarily technical concern.

Governance is necessarily multi-stakeholder in nature

The earlier revelations that national governments hold a fringe, limited role in Internet governance may surprise many readers, but it is ultimately a consequence of the above point about governance as a technical rather than political necessity. With cyberspace resulting from the fruits of many technical innovations, a true product of collaborative research ventures across decades, governance too was only ever going to continue in the same vein by following this collaborative and multi-stakeholder nature.

Never was a tool going to enjoy the levels of growth and empowerment that cyberspace and, specifically, the Internet did without encouraging and enabling the participation of as many users as possible. If Isaacson is correct to state that public awareness is an important component of innovation,[102] then it is simply inconceivable that the ubiquity achieved by the Internet could have happened without at the same time generating a multistakeholder governance model to support it. Under no terms could it be envisioned that the development of cyberspace would be at present levels of scale and user penetration were governance to have been approached in a different format, particularly any model that would be by definition exclusionary in any way. Even if a multilateral nation-led approach had been taken and was considered in any kind of counter-factual history, one could easily contend that the Internet's spread would not have happened as fast for a simple reason; growth was dictated by technical capabilities and not based on political belief sets during the late 1980s and throughout the 1990s. National, politically led programs would have lacked the technical knowledge and commercial efficiency to roll out the Internet with the same effects and success. Indeed, this was a motivating factor in the Clinton administration's decision to devolve governance to the private sector in the first place.[103]

From the (albeit relatively short) history of cyberspace and the Internet to date, it is quite clear that the multi-stakeholder model has been successful, indeed shockingly so, at balancing the disparate needs of not only the sheer scale of interested parties, but so too their differing natures. For a model to operate globally, incorporating technical as well as political concerns, ranging from the individual, through the corporate and up to the nation state as well as international bodies, is a marvel to behold in and of itself. As the creation of cyberspace and the Internet was born out of collaborative zeal that ranged across numerous different sciences, so too must governance be a collaborative, multi-stakeholder effort; the history of governance to date supports this as a defining characteristic.

Internet governance has remained apolitical

If Internet governance was determined by technical necessity over the political, bringing its scholarly nature of collaborative multi-stakeholderism with it from the realms of science and engineering, then it is a direct consequence that so far Internet governance has remained an apolitical affair. That this is so is due to two factors, one that is technical and not political, and one that is very much political as well as being an accident of history at the same time.

First, the apolitical nature of governance to date is due to the speed of technical advancement that has enabled cyberspace to explode and for the Internet to achieve global ubiquity. Simply put, the dynamic is that technological progress has so outpaced the abilities of nation states and law-making bodies to keep up that they are forever caught in a catch-up loop. A key determining factor in making the Internet too valuable to prevent or challenge politically is an economic imperative; with the global economy having already become reliant on the cyberspace system before the World Wide Web brought in the masses, it was inevitable that the spread would be encouraged. This spread ensured that the Western capitalist economic model could flourish even further, providing governments with only a positive reason to encourage the continued spread.

Alongside this technical advancement was of course the accompanying professional requirements to both staff and govern this space. Indeed, throughout its entire existence, cyberspace has been necessarily governed by those with the requisite professional knowledge to decide intelligently on what was necessary for it to operate on the technical – both physical and logical – level. By governing according to the technical requirements of the space, technical expertise would logically become the core characteristic required to qualify anybody to govern.

The second reason for the apolitical nature of governance is indeed a political one. This reason is that the explosion of cyberspace and the Internet into a globally accessible tool occurred at the height of the Western liberal triumph. Simply put, by coinciding with the historically rare occurrence of a major triumph of one political order over another, the Internet was able to grow without being challenged by any different political vision. Cyberspace, and the Internet especially, were born as an ultimate expression of liberal individualism; few other innovations can be argued to carry the same impact on the individual as the Internet combined with the PC has brought. One may argue that the printing press is the prime contender, but this author would favour the Internet for the reason that the printing press landed at a time when a small proportion of humanity commanded any literacy, unlike the global population that the Internet was thrust upon in the 1990s.

The liberal order had triumphed in the Cold War, with the happy (for the West, at least) accident that the most potent tool for the spread of and access to information was about to be unleashed on the world. Quite simply, the apolitical governance model enjoyed by the Internet to date is as much thanks to the triumph of its parent political order – liberalism – as it is to the technical innovations that also leave policy- and law-makers struggling to keep up. Lewis is right to note that a mixture of libertarianism, anti-authoritarianism, and belief in a New Economy were central fixtures in how the early Internet flourished in this way.[104] This enabled a permissive political environment for an apolitical governance structure to root itself in and prosper without significant political challenge.

The current model is now subject to political challenge

Although how the model has been apolitical to date has just been detailed, care has also been taken to reveal how this apolitical characteristic is ironically thanks to the permissive political conditions created by the victory of the liberal world order in the Cold War. The apolitical model simply rode the soaring stock of liberalism, creating the impression that this approach would remain unchallenged, which is very much no longer the case.

The full details of the challenges brought to the way of running global cyberspace will be fully explored in the next section, as it is far too extensive for immediate treatment here, yet it is important to note here that there is of course a delicate balance between naivety and optimism in the apolitical approach. For those of the Western liberal persuasion, the apolitical multi-stakeholder governance model inspires optimism that it may not only long continue, but indeed prove to be permanently enduring as not only a superior model, but also the only viable one. For others, however, including even those in the West, such a view can be viewed as hopelessly naive, a romantic delusion born of the permissive climate of the 1990s where an apolitical approach could be indulged, for a time. This view was perhaps always naive to think that it would continue forever without encountering political challenge from both within and without, as is now the case.

While the next section will fully detail the challenges that have emerged from without – from differing political positions entirely to the liberal model – challenges have also emerged from within the liberal model that are worth briefly noting here. That this is so is because of the security issues that cyberspace has brought over its early decades of use; the rise of cybercrime in particular – be it state-level espionage against Western corporations or individual acts of blackmail, theft, sexual exploitation, drug trafficking and the like – has created a need among even those nations who birthed the Internet and the World Wide Web to establish stronger political control over this space. The specific examples of the United States, the United Kingdom (exactly those who birthed the key innovations), and the European Union go far to revealing the seriousness that democratic governments attach to tackling the problems of cyber security domestically.

   In the United States, a core example was the notable case of the Federal Bureau of Investigation (FBI) trying to force the technology giant Apple to assist it in breaching its iPhone encryption in order to aid the investigation of the San Bernardino attack in 2015. This led to a standoff between the corporate world and government, where in this case it was actually the private business of Apple who based their refusal to help the FBI on the protection of individual liberty. The essence of Apple's argument was that any "backdoor" created would irreparably damage encryption, rendering it no longer end-to-end, and would therefore compromise the security and privacy of all Apple users. This position led to Apple CEO Tim Cook being labelled by *The Economist* as "The Privacy Martyr" on its front cover.[105] With the court case between the FBI and Apple being dropped, a lack of resolution between state access past encryption, individual liberty, and the state's power to coerce private companies to assist it remains unresolved.[106] It remains however, a fascinating if brief skirmish between the state and big power over a problem that will not resolve itself.

   In the United Kingdom, a similar skirmish has also occurred in recent times, following the public debate over encryption after the Westminster Bridge terror attack in 2017. The use of end-to-end encrypted apps like WhatsApp has led to the British home secretary, Amber Rudd, to call for government access past such encryption much in the same manner as the American federal government had sought to achieve in its battle with Apple. Much like the FBI in America, Amber Rudd found herself on the end of criticisms that both she and the British government had failed to achieve even a basic level of technological understanding. Britain and America have found themselves in a catch-22 position of making the case for state security whereby, subject to rightful judicial process, interception of communications can be lawfully granted in extremis. In 2015, at a joint press conference with President Barack Obama, Prime Minister David Cameron stated, 'we're not asking for backdoors (in encryption). We believe in very clear front doors through legal processes that should help to keep our countries safe.'[107] This is at the same time accepting that fast-paced technological innovations impose unpalatable and perhaps even unsolvable security problems upon policy-makers.

In the European Union, meanwhile, the focus has now become one of protecting individual privacy by returning control of data to individuals, through the recently established General Data Protection Regulation, which went live on 25 May 2018. At the time of writing, the biggest target of efforts to put big tech in check has been Facebook; this has been most vividly seen via the implication of the social media giant in playing a key role in facilitating Russian active measures to interfere with the 2016 presidential election.[108] Facebook CEO Mark Zuckerberg has already made a memorable appearance to the US Congress in April 2018 that included apologies for the company's failing to police numerous areas of misuse of the platform.[109] Since that appearance, Facebook has become increasingly embattled, with accusations of a business practice that is centred around 'delay, deny and deflect'[110] through Zuckerberg courting the fury of numerous other nations by refusing to appear personally as he has before Congress to an international inquiry[111] on Facebook's activities.[112] What the case of Facebook makes plain, however, is that for any company whose business model is fundamentally based on the acquisition and use of data, stringent imposition of law and regulation is coming as a reassertion of political authority. The statement made in the opening to the congressional hearing by Republican Rep. Greg Walden sums up the dynamic well: 'I think it is time to ask whether Facebook may have moved too fast and broken too many things.'[113]

To conclude this section, while it has been shown that Internet governance as we know it has been a very apolitical affair, there is a strong reassertion of political authority that is already well underway, as various early skirmishes with tech giants have proven. Now that political challenge has been established, it is time to turn full attention to the return of politics into cyberspace.

1.3 The return of politics

> The road to a world order may be long and uncertain, but no meaningful progress can be made if one of the most pervasive elements of international life is excluded from dialogue.[114]

Kissinger outlines perfectly a core reason for the return of politics in discourse on addressing the insecurities brought by cyberspace; the effects of cyberspace and the Internet have no doubt been highly beneficial globally, but the risks also present a serious challenge to the apolitical character it has been conducted with to date. As Kissinger convincingly states, order

cannot be maintained if cyberspace remains excluded from political dialogue; politics must return for the future of cyberspace to be safeguarded.
The purpose of the previous section was to outline how we have reached
where we are with Internet governance, concluding that it has been a largely
apolitical affair due to the unique characteristics of cyberspace combined
with the historical coincidence of the liberal world order's triumph in the
Cold War. This chapter needs to conclude, however, by rounding off the
story of how we have reached the state of *insecurity* that now prevails in
cyberspace, which involves detailing the return of politics into the equation
as the primary point of inquiry here. Before exploring the return of politics
in depth, it is necessary to recount briefly the importance of historical context in facilitating cyberspace's brief apolitical honeymoon.

The liberal triumph

Why was cyberspace able to enjoy global growth and be effectively unhin-
dered by the concerns of state politics? It was shown above that the Clinton
administration, in their decision to leave Internet governance as a matter
for the private sector, had effectively protected cyberspace by ensuring it
would be free of such concerns. The greater question behind this decision
was, however, why was President Clinton able to do this without effective
challenge? The answer lies with the victory of liberalism in the Cold War.

The exact longevity of the struggle of liberalism against competing orders
is certainly one of considerable debate within historical circles, with traditional historical accounts generally separating the struggles of liberalism
against fascist totalitarianism and communist totalitarianism respectively –
carrying as it does the weight of Cold War literature that is far beyond being
able to be cited here.[115] Others conflate liberalism's struggle as a single episode, preferring to weave a historical meta-narrative. Philip Bobbitt is certainly of the latter camp, with his position that the war that began in 1914
only ended in 1990, representing the 'Long War of the Nation State.'[116]
Delving deeper into this fascinating terrain of unique historical contexts and
episodes versus historical meta-narratives is clearly beyond the scope of
this work, the point at this stage is instead to highlight that no matter which
position of that particular debate one adopts, there is unmistakable agreement that the end of the Cold War marked a momentous point in human
political history, and one that carries greater importance to the evolution of
cyberspace and cyber security than it has before been granted.

So powerful was the collapse of the communist totalitarian challenge to
the liberal order that one scholar was so bold as to declare an "end to history" itself.[117] As common – indeed all but clichéd – as Fukuyama's position has become all the way down to junior undergraduates in International

Relations, his position very accurately captures the essence of the historical reason behind cyberspace's ability to enjoy an apolitical youth. In declaring that 'liberal democracy remains the only coherent political aspiration that spans different regions and cultures around the globe,'[118] it seemed clear that there was no political challenger to liberalism. Buzan is also useful in reminding us all that those who made this liberal argument, absent any serious intellectual competition at the time, came to also believe wholeheartedly that where 'a liberal economic order prevails, states will be less inclined to use force.'[119] Such momentous historical events, powered by these beliefs, resulted in the decade of the 1990s becoming a 'liberal moment.'[120] That moment happened to coincide with the technological convergence of the PC, the Internet, and the World Wide Web; protected by the absence of any serious political rival of note and birthed by the victors of the liberal order, the fragile infancy of cyberspace took place during what can be best described as an apolitical honeymoon, those halcyon days of the early post-Cold War years. It is almost astonishing to this author that this contextual coincidence has remained absent from the literature on cyber security to date, for it is clearly a vital contextual element in how cyberspace developed, as argued here.

Why has politics returned?

The argument must be apparent to readers; the apolitical honeymoon enjoyed by cyberspace to date is over, but why? If the liberal victory was indeed so complete, it begs the question, why has politics returned? To put the argument simply, a political challenge was inevitable, both from within and from without.

The answer lies in two arguments posed here; first, that the emergence of multipolarity and the relative erosion (or balancing) of American power has created the space for arguments that indeed already existed in the 1990s to benefit from real political backing. Second, the course of events in cyberspace have presented serious and genuine security concerns that can no longer be ignored; these can be roughly broken down into two realms of events, cybercrime and cyber-enabled/connected revolutions across the world. The former has perturbed Western nations most of all, who are now challenged to protect their own hyper-connected societies from harm. The latter, meanwhile, concerns above all autocracies – Russia and China especially – who have viewed events such as the Arab Spring and Colour revolutions as mortal threats enabled by Internet-connected devices and services.

On multipolarity, right away realism must strike in asserting that no notion of an end to history could have been expected to endure. To have believed so was no doubt an exercise in hopeful naivety at best and, at worst, a state of romanticised political delusion, born of the permissive climate of the 1990s where a belief in unipolarity, liberal triumphalism, and, consequently, apolitical Internet governance *could* be indulged.

Any serious student and scholar of history is all too aware of the transitory nature of hegemonic rule, however long it may be established. A precursor case to consider is the fate of the British Empire; bookshelves groan under the weight of those who debate the notion of the *Pax Britannica*, arguing numerous cases for when exactly the British decline occurred.[121] This case has also begun to motivate concerns about relative American – and therefore liberal – decline since the 1990s.

Returning to Ikenberry's views is essential at this stage, for he rightly notes that despite holding a position of hegemony unrivalled in history,[122] the structures on which American power have been built are suffering from erosion: 'it has the capacity to dominate the world, but not the legitimacy to rule. It has power but not authority.'[123] If Ikenberry is right on both counts, the situation of the early twenty-first century was inevitably going to invite political challenge from some, if not many, quarters, and on many political fronts. And, like the case with the British Empire, questions abound among scholars as to how durable American global hegemony and leadership will prove to be; Kagan questions the notion of decline as an inevitability, offering the optimistic argument that America in the present moment commands more influence on the future than any other contender in history,[124] but that it faces the choice of what it will do. Krepinevich seconds this view in imaginatively calling for greater innovation in the military, stating 'The choice is ours. Time is growing short.'[125] Ferguson, meanwhile, suggests that America suffers from three chronic deficits that impedes its ability to lead and answers Kagan's and Krepinevich's views of choice – economic, manpower, and attention.[126] Despite this, Ferguson is clear in his insistence that there should be, in his words, a 'liberal empire' that America works to lead and maintain.[127]

Regardless of the truth to the outstanding questions of American decline, one cannot contest that *relative* decline is in effect, due to the rise of multipolarity in the global system. Several events have occurred in the early twenty-first century that have, if not compromised, then certainly tarnished elements of America's status as the sole hyper power; two will be cited for the purposes of this argument. The first instance is the tarnishing of moral authority after 9/11; the resulting military campaigns[128] following the attacks of 11 September 2001, particularly the war in Iraq, went far in removing America's claim to moral authority, given the division of opinion among its allies, the failure to find weapons of mass destruction, and abuses such as at Abu Ghraib. Simply put, the pursuit of liberal foreign policies could no longer credibly claim to be completely benevolent. Second, the economic collapse of 2008 seemed to have fractured the superiority of the liberal economic order based on capitalism;[129] with the economies of the liberal world remaining in deep periods of recovery and imposed austerity, the economic might of America is no longer seen as what it once was. In this latter case, America has been either (or both) unable or unwilling to underwrite global recovery as it once did with the Marshall Plan[130] after the Second World War.

Multipolarity is therefore rising across the global system, not because of any fatal compromise of the structures of American power beyond repair, but thanks to the cumulative consequences of numerous events globally. Brzezinski is correct to state that the cumulative effect of these events was to confirm a self-evident geopolitical reality: 'the consequential shift in the centre of gravity of global power and economic dynamism from the Atlantic toward the Pacific, from the West toward the East.'[131] With that shift came the more forceful articulation of challenges to the liberal worldview, concerns that were never really absent in concerns about cyberspace but had merely been overrun by a more powerful America in the 1990s. Raustiala wisely reminds readers that the multilateral counterargument from China and others regarding how to govern cyberspace was present in the mid-1990s;[132] now that the balance of power is shifting once more, old positions have simply surfaced anew.

The second reason behind the return of politics lies in the passage of events, which have introduced significant security concerns. In particular, it is argued here that the rise of cybercrime, and cyber-enabled revolutions, are respectively the key events driving the return of politics among nation states. Cybercrime is most notably driving Western concerns, with revolutions – particularly the fear of succumbing to one – concerning non-liberal nations.

Cybercrime

Cybercrime and other uses of cyberspace for nefarious activities have become a core concern in Western countries, with private industry and scholarship alike struggling to keep up with the surge of data in this arena. Even a cursory Google check of government, industry, and academic sources will reveal veritable mountains of analytics trying to prize out key trends and meanings. Major providers of cyber security solutions produce multiple detailed reports per year – a basic exploration will take researchers to products such as Symantec's *Internet Security Threat Report*,[133] Hewlett Packard's *Cyber Risk Report*[134] or *State of Security Operations*,[135] NTT's *Global Threat Intelligence Report*,[136] or Microsoft's *Security Intelligence*

Report,[137] among dozens of other competing private bodies – indeed, even identifying the trends in cybercrime is a key analytic imperative in order to try and shift correct defensive attention to the latest threats. Core trends in this regard have involved the activity of cybercrime migrating across different tactics. Hewlett Packard labelled 2014 the 'year of the breach,'[138] whereas the NTT Group noted DoS/DDoS attacks falling some 39% in 2015[139] compared to 2014, preferring to move to other attack methods. Symantec focused on a core trend in 2015 that a 36% increase in unique malware strand variants were detected compared to the year before.[140] Since 2016, it has been the rise of ransomware that has taken cybercrime from growing trends like that spotted by Kaspersky – a 17.7% rise of users encountering ransomware between 2015 and 2016[141] – to being the preferred tool of choice in the world's first global cyber attacks in 2017, specifically the WannaCry and Petya/Not-Petya ransomware attacks that impacted an eclectic mix of victims globally. The British government's Department for Culture, Media, and Sport in their 2018 Cyber Security Breaches Survey[142] found that 43% of all businesses and 19% of all charities in the UK had suffered some kind of cyber breach between 2017 and 2018. And this variety of sources and positions is before one even considers the presence of large consultancy firms like Deloitte and PwC with their frequent analytic produce in this space.

The point of this admittedly shallow foray into the avalanche of cybercrime data is not to exhaustively deal with, or even comprehensively summarise, the detail of cybercrime trends, but simply to illustrate the clear spikes in cybercrime that have happened globally and have been increasingly reported and analysed throughout the second decade of the twenty-first century. Especially pertinent is the realisation 'that your average cyber attacker will be part of an organisation that is far closer to a corporate enterprise in its structure.'[143] It is instead the impact of cybercrime that is most important; the scale of harm varies, of course, depending on exactly where in the world one looks, but the impact of cybercrime economically has become simply too high, so much so that politically it cannot be ignored.

This impact has been quantified by McAfee in their 2018 report on the impact of cybercrime. In that report, they state that the global cost of cybercrime has increased to $600 billion globally,[144] a staggering figure. That report also notes problems in its data set, such as a failure to report crime, with McAfee citing the UK estimate that only 13% of suspected cybercrime is ever reported.[145] A core takeaway from this is not only the quantified cost McAfee has produced, but also the certainty that this is not the true number because of lack of reportage of cybercrime. Instances of cybercrime are so frequent, outlets such as *Wired* even run pieces on the worst hacks or breaches of the year with almost alarming regularity. With cybercrime having become a genuine business killer and a risk that is trans-industrial in nature, it is short wonder why it has garnered such political attention in the democracies.

Cyber espionage

Taking the UK as an example, the decision in 2015 to establish a National Cyber Security Centre (NCSC) under the charge of the signals intelligence service GCHQ, is a clear recognition by the British government of the severity of risks posed by cybercrime. In the 2011–2015 UK Cyber Security Strategy, the lead objective was for the UK 'to tackle cybercrime and be one of the most secure places in the world to do business in cyberspace.'[146] Britain had correctly recognised that its security in cyberspace is intrinsically linked with its economic prosperity, and that focus needed to be geared towards cybercrime in particular. This is a view that has also been added to by the continued debates regarding government ability to access encryption (dealt with earlier in section 1.2).

In the American example, while cybercrime has been certainly as potent as elsewhere in the world, the key driver has been its particular criminal use to facilitate corporate espionage and intellectual property theft. The suspicion against such theft has been overwhelmingly focused on the Chinese state as the perpetrator or at least active supporter. Indeed, there is a litany of case studies and incidents dating back almost two decades of this type of economic espionage being carried out, with many carrying unique identifier campaign monikers, the accumulation of which has itself presented a veritable phone book to lose readers in; from Titan Rain in 2003–05 (a series of coordinated breaches against US government targets), Operation Night Dragon in 2009 (systematic intrusions against American and European oil companies), Operation Aurora in 2009–10 (a highly sophisticated and targeted attack against Google), and Operation Shady Rat in 2011[147] (targeting the International Olympic Committee and World Anti-Doping Agency before and after the 2008 Beijing Olympics), among others. Shakarian argues that when one considers the attacks simply across their timeline, such thefts show 'a definite progression in sophistication.'[148]

Beyond these are the numerous and pervasive suspicions of individual government and corporate cases, such as persistent breaches of the fifth generation F-35 fighter program globally since perhaps 2006[149] (Lockheed Martin and British Aerospace are the best known victims); the placing of logic bombs in the US electrical grid in 2009;[150] the compromise of Coca-Cola's systems in 2009;[151] the penetration of servers in the US Chamber of Commerce in 2011;[152] intrusion into the sensitive files of NASA's Jet Propulsion Laboratory in 2012;[153] the data theft suffered by the US Office of Personnel Management from 2012;[154] the covert instalment of malware into CCleaner products in 2017;[155] the breach and theft of IP from the Naval Undersea Warfare Centre in 2018;[156] and Bloomberg's late-2018 claim of penetration of Apple's fundamental supply chain[157] that has been so strongly denied by the tech giant that they even took the unusual step of sending a letter to the US Congress to issue their rebuttal.[158]

The list of corporate and government breaches goes on, and far beyond American interests as well. The key point to establish is that cyber espionage activities are a core concern for many actors, especially the United States but not uniquely so. Indeed, the concern is mirrored in the UK, with the NCSC issuing guidance to telecommunications companies not to use Chinese firm ZTE's products in their infrastructure. Specifically, Technical Director Levy states that 'the national security risks arising from the use of ZTE equipment or services within the context of the existing UK telecommunications infrastructure cannot be mitigated.'[159]

Such aggressive targeting of American intellectual property, technological pre-eminence, and governmental structures was seen as such a problem it resulted in a state-level agreement between presidents Obama and Xi Jinping in 2015 to try and curb such activities. Of this, President Obama said that 'neither the US or the Chinese Government will conduct or knowingly support cyber-enabled theft of intellectual property, including trade secrets or other confidential business information for commercial advantage.'[160] The agreement led to something of a decline in activity for a period with a noticeable drop in American cases,[161] yet was immediately viewed in some quarters with critique[162] and has since been challenged as under constant strain with Chinese behaviour evolving.[163] With the transition of office from presidents Obama to Trump, the agreement is now largely seen as defunct, with Chinese espionage efforts having reconstituted and indeed accelerated in practice once more.[164]

The impact of cyber espionage activities in this way is creating increased global tension in two ways, according to Singer and Friedman. First, 'it reinforces a sense that not everyone in the world marketplace is playing by the same set of rules.'[165] Second, 'this theft threatens nations' long-term economic security.'[166] The conduct of cybercrime – both through common criminality simply enabled by cyber means and through much more expansive espionage penetrating the fabric of innovative research, corporate secrets, and the conduct of government – have created severe concern among the Western democracies exactly as Singer and Friedman argue. President Obama's 2015 remark that cyberspace was a sort of 'wild, wild West'[167] captures the Western fear well, the fear that motivates the return of politics this author argues for. That fear is that while cyberspace brings untold societal advantages, nations have become so intrinsically dependent that a corresponding vulnerability is afforded. And, without the reassertion of politics to secure this space, long-term security (in its many guises) will be compromised.

Cyber revolutions

For the authoritarian states, however, the prime concern is not cybercrime (although it is certainly a concern for them too) but cyber-enabled or -enhanced revolutions. Klimburg is correct in his assertion that 'authoritarian states have long since viewed their principle security threat as arising from "informational effects," that is, the infiltration of problematic political messages.'[168] Two of Kello's disruptive features of cyberspace lie at the heart of this reasoning on the part of authoritarian states: 'the expansion of nonphysical threats to national security, the growing ability of non-state actors to instigate diplomatic and military crises.'[169] The chief concern of an authoritarian regime is always retaining absolute control of the domestic populace, the securing of the regime above all else. Howard French describes the Chinese dynamic well: 'China's political system operates out of an instinctive distrust of the people it administers.'[170] Historically, this has been chiefly achieved via strict control of the information flows and the imposition of the state's narrative, reinforced through regular and brutal oppression. If the underlying view of the world as espoused by the regime is able to be challenged because of access to contradictory information, then the very notion of authority in a regime is subject to challenge; the possibility of such challenge growing and nurturing into holding popular appeal is the essence of fear from authoritarian regimes to cyberspace.

The cases of both Russia and China are the most important to consider, as the chief challengers to the Western liberal order itself, as well as their representing the specific "Cyber Sovereignty" challenge to the Western view for the future of cyberspace. These states always regarded the Internet 'as a potential threat from the outset,'[171] and their view of this has only been reinforced by a particular series of events – the Arab Spring, the first demonstration of how the Internet had 'rewritten the street protest playbook.'[172] The immediate spark for the Arab Spring originated in Tunisia on 17 December 2010; when a police officer ignominiously confiscated his produce cart, Mohammed Bouazizi set himself on fire in protest. Bouazizi's act of self-immolation initially led to riots in his Tunisian hometown, but this very quickly spread to wider Tunisia and then the MENA region as a whole. Uprisings were catalysed in Bahrain, Egypt, Syria, Yemen, and Jordan, leading in some cases to a replacement of leadership.

The most notable cases were the collapse of President Zine el-Abidine bin Ali's regime of 23 years in Tunisia; President Hosni Mubarak of

Egypt eventually resigning due to the pressure of protests in places like Tahrir Square; and Yemen's President Ali Abdullah Saleh stepping down after 33 years in power. Within these movements, the role of social media platforms – Twitter especially – has garnered much attention given the speed of movement that the Arab Spring wrought across the region. Howard and Duffy et al. argue that social media played a central role in shaping debate during the Arab Spring, with online discussions occurring prior to significant events on the ground. They further argue that social media was a key enabler in helping the spread of the movement so fast, 'helping spread democratic ideas across international borders.'[173]

It is, of course, necessary to temper somewhat the assertions regarding how decisive social media was to the Arab Spring, which is where Dewey and Kaden et al.'s Stanford report prepared for the American Defense Intelligence Agency (DIA) is useful. There they argue that social media proved a useful but not necessary tool for mobilising the protests seen,[174] highlighting that other major contributing factors underpinned the reason for popular discontent. Despite this tempering, however, they do note some core conclusions on the role of social media worth, quoting at length here:

> Social media's ability to offer membership in virtual civil society groups we believe boosted participation in protests, highlighting the importance the tool played in facilitating social unrest. Social media also increased international attention to local events in MENA, which may have raised morale and increased pressure on local governments.[175]

Armed with social media, individuals approach what Patrikarakos terms *homo digitalis*, 'the hyper empowered individual, networked, globally-connected, and more potent than ever before' in dismantling traditional hierarchies of both media and information flows.[176] Whatever the degree of impact that social media had – whether it approaches this vision Patrikarakos argues for or is simply a useful tool – its significance remains a topic of debate in academic circles; what is in no doubt, however, is the fear that has been highlighted in the minds of other authoritarian regimes faced with the possibility of *homo digitalis*. Lindsey is most helpful in this regard, in stating that what social media has actually done is to help 'weaponise information down to the individual level.'[177]

An individual armed with uncontrolled access to information that can subvert the official view, the state-agreed truth of the world, is an existential threat to an authoritarian regime. The events of the Arab Spring certainly were not lost on either Moscow or Beijing, who have in turn presented intriguing reactions as to how to cope with the threat posed by elements such as social media. These reactions come in two broad strategies, from

China, the appropriation of tech tools in order to establish sovereign dominance over the individual, a reassertion on information flows. From Russia, meanwhile, the primary effort has been a progressive campaign to undermine truth, exploiting the reality of the sheer volume and availability of information without routine scrutiny in an effort to sow confusion and mistrust in reality itself. Both approaches, unfortunately for those of a liberal mindset, are proving highly successful in application.

China: The Social Credit System

China is already in the pilot stage of what is termed the Social Credit System, which has been in place since 2014 and is scheduled to become mandatory on a national scale in 2020. According to the Chinese state, the purpose of this system is to build a 'sincerity culture'[178] that encourages traditional values in society. Furthermore, it is argued as a necessity due to China's historic lack of a credit rating system like those that underpin much of Western financial approaches. Yet there is concern that there are far darker purposes to the system, building 'a high-tech authoritarian future'[179] instead of a system purely for the financial interest of Chinese citizens.

In truth, such a system requires only a few twists in the West to become a reality. The risks of "over-sharing" on social media platforms like Facebook and Twitter are regular topics of privacy debates, with the charity Privacy International including social media intelligence (SOCMINT) as one of its topic areas.[180] When citizens have for years freely given up disproportionate data to loyalty schemes, search engines, retailers, and media organisations who in turn have been selling that data to advertisers, among others, it stands to reason that there would be other actors who seek other applications for the abundance of data on offer.

The Social Credit System is aimed at 'strengthening the sincerity consciousness of the members of society,'[181] an oblique way of saying raising trust between societal members but based on a citizen's score. It is this scoring of individuals that gets to the heart of why the Social Credit System carries such dark undercurrents; notionally, scoring is for the purposes of establishing financial credit, much like evaluation systems in the West. But a closer look at the methods behind scoring quickly reveal that the information being gathered is excessive to this purpose, and that its scoring applications also go much further than a simple assessment of the individual's financial risk.

Under the pilot scheme, underwritten by Sesame Credit, the individual can be measured against a score between 350 and 950. There are five categories that influence this score: "credit history" is first, the actual financial performance of an individual in paying back loans, not defaulting on rent etc. Second is "fulfilment capacity," which is a way of monitoring the individual's history and ability to 'fulfil his or her contractual obligations' more widely. "Personal characteristics" is the third category, involving the verification of what in the West is termed personally identifiable information like full name, address, contact details, passport numbers, and the like. The fourth category is where things become clearly disproportionate, which is "personal characteristics." This is based on, as an easy example, the shopping preferences of the individual and is used to judge them accordingly. Under this logic, the purchase of socially approved products can lead to a better score, whereas the purchase of items seen as undesirable or socially questionable could hurt the score.[182] The fifth and final category is "interpersonal relationships," meaning the individual's choice of friends and social relationships.[183] Importantly, however, this could easily include your non-choices – broader family connections and colleagues, school classmates, perhaps even one's dating history. Judgement by association, however loosely associated, under this system carries wider ramifications than at first appears on the surface.

Such categories naturally at this stage beg the question, what do users get? Very simply one's scoring rank conveys access to societal necessities, "special privileges" based on one's trustworthiness. Botsman details that when a score of 600 is reached, the user can take out a basic loan; reach 650 and they can rent a car without leaving a deposit. At 700, they can apply for travel to Singapore without supporting documents; hit 750 and 'they get fast-tracked to a coveted pan-European Schengen visa.'[184] Access to dating sites has also been attempted, with trials whereby scores of 750 and above give men access to exclusive singles on Alipay.[185] By establishing control over the individual's need to access finance and travel, through to their desires and hopes for travel and the possibility of a family, one can immediately see the level of control that can be established over the individual through dominance of this information flow.

The input into the system is based on technology we all know very well indeed. First of all are the traditional components of public surveillance, CCTV; Oliver Moody notes in a special for UK newspaper *The Times* that only nine years ago China had installed only half the CCTV cameras that Britain does (some 2.7 million), yet by 2020 is forecast to have somewhere in the region of 400 million in place.[186] The proliferation of body-mounted cameras on public officials – be they police officers, postal workers, or train conductors – adds a mobile layer to this system before one comes to the most ubiquitous element of all, the smartphone. With the data and communications from over 700 million smartphones (and climbing) being both volunteered by users and compelled from app and service providers, input is carried right down to the individual at all times. Yet this is simply the input; as Moody rightly states, the most insidious part of the system is that which remains unseen: the algorithms that to most are beyond comprehension and reproach. 'The idea is not only to know the whereabouts and doings of all the people, all the time. It is to be able to predict where they will go and what they will do in the future.'[187] Worry permeates so deeply in Western research on the bias indirectly written into algorithms that little thought has been given to *deliberately* biased code created with specific political purposes in mind. In China, the unaccountable and unchallengeable code that underpin the Social Credit System most definitely fits O'Neill's categorisation of the algorithm that is itself a 'Weapon of Math Destruction.'[188]

This is an intriguing, yet also entirely logical, pairing of the state-level desire for social control with the promise that technology brings. Instead of relying purely on the historic methods of authoritarian oppression, this is a method of social control that exploits the very technology that individuals both demand and depend on, creating a reward-points system in return; as Botsman succinctly says, 'It's gamified obedience.'[189] Yet even Botsman fails to probe the truly dark possibilities of where such a system may lie, only acknowledging that the "losers" in such a system may be disadvantaged only to the limit of being provided poor Internet connectivity and having restricted access to travel, even dining out.[190] Moody comes somewhat closer in stating that the 'silence from the losers is deafening' and that self-censorship is being automated.[191] Where greater questioning must lead, however, is to recognise that for all those who establish their "trustworthiness" to the state another question is raised, what happens to those who fail to do this? The Social Credit System will not only disadvantage many in society and create incredible segregation and inequality across all walks of life, it may also present the Chinese state with a ready-made target list of the "undesirables" in society or, as it more likely to be the parlance in this system, the "untrustworthy."

One's imagination needs not stretch very far, particularly given Europe's twentieth-century history – to recognise the possibilities afforded by a centralised registration of society's "untrusted" individuals, who pose any kind of subversive threat to the 'sincerity culture' that China is attempting to build. The database would surely be used by state security services, in an almost *Minority Report*-esque scenario, to identify threats to the state before they ever even achieve conscious recognition of their own activities (whether real or imagined), based on their reading habits, social acquaintances, and perhaps even hobbies. If one wishes to know how China seeks to avoid their own Arab Spring and prevent a Tiananmen Square armed with smartphones and social media, look to the Social Credit System, for it aims to sleepwalk Chinese citizens into an echo chamber of obedience with a points reward system. This is a key milestone for China securing itself from within in cyberspace.

Russia: My Truth Against Yours[192]

> The very disrespect of Russians for objective truth – indeed, their *disbelief in its existence* – leads them to view all stated facts as instruments for furtherance of one ulterior purpose or another.[193]

Reaching back to the wisdom of George Kennan's legendary long telegram helps to remind all of a systemic truth to the Russian view of the world, an inherent disbelief in the notion of objective truth that long predated the creation of cyberspace. Russian activities in cyberspace are so illustrative precisely because they reveal to all how a novel, new space has been strategically appropriated for traditional political beliefs on the part of the Russians. Thanks in large measure to the aggressive reassertion of Russian power internationally in the second decade of the twenty-first century – through aggressive aerial manoeuvres close to NATO airspace,[194] submarine operations in Swedish waters,[195] the annexation of Crimea and intervention in Ukraine, and exotic assassination attempts in Britain,[196] to name but a few – media outlets regularly question whether there is a new Cold War in place or at least brewing.[197]

A better understanding of the Russian view lies again in revisiting Kennan, to acknowledge that at the heart of their 'neurotic view of world affairs is traditional and instinctive Russian sense of insecurity.'[198] While it is little more than media headline grabbing to assert that today's situation matches the level of confrontation that the Cold War was, it does make sense to show an element of analytic empathy to the Russian worldview. This view is better characterised as one that accepted its Cold War defeat,[199] but never accepted that its struggle with the West and the United States was over. Ostrovsky captures this dynamic well in detailing that, unlike their forebears at the start of the Cold War who were at least shaped by the victory of the Second World War, the current ruling elite of Russia 'were shaped by what they consider to be their loss of the Cold War, and their feeling of rejection by the West' that has led to the triumph of a strange 'mixture of hostility and jealousy.'[200] This pathological disbelief in objective truth combined, oddly, with a firm real belief that the struggle with the liberal West continues serve to provide the prime motivators for how Russia has begun to make use of cyberspace, a central element in the post-Cold War struggle with the United States:[201] to attack truth itself.

In order to detail exactly how Russia has made use of information operations, one could reach back both near and far in history for examples, so prevalent is its practice. More recent cases that won't be considered here are those of the 2007 and 2008 campaigns on Estonia and Georgia, for they are very well understood at this stage.[202] Instead, attention will briefly focus on three key contemporary cases that illustrate exactly how far Russian exploitation of cyber tools has come: Ukraine since 2014, the US presidential election in 2016, and the attempted assassination of Sergei Skripal in the UK in 2018. Russian operations in Ukraine since 2014 have, very justifiably, resulted in an avalanche of political, strategic, and scholarly interest. The arrival of "little green men," as they were labelled in Western media circles, but "polite men" by Moscow, mere "volunteers" who formed local "self-defence groups,"[203] signalled a new problem with consequences far beyond Ukraine itself: a testing of the boundaries of truth and how far credulity could be stretched while engaging in the pursuit of strategic interests. The traditional Russian geopolitical interest in Ukraine matters less here than their use of that country increasingly as a "test lab"[204] for novel cyber tactics, including the manipulation of public opinion 'before an insurrection in Zaporizhzia, wresting the region from the orbit of the central government in Kiev.'[205] Kremlin leaks that the UK newspaper *The Times* reported on details a toolkit for what is now termed Russian hybrid warfare. Although Giles effectively covers the linguistic difficulties of the term when applied to Russia, accepting that it is imperfect,[206] it is effective enough to highlight that 'For Moscow, hackers, trolls, hired thugs, political "technologists" and paid-for protesters are more useful than tanks, planes, and soldiers.'[207]

Central to this is the desire to manipulate public debate through a constant campaign of disinformation, incredulous denials, and a subversion of facts. Giles notes that Western media outlets struggled until the end of 2014 to realise that they were the target of a concerted campaign of subversion and will still unwittingly report Russian disinformation as fact.[208] Wirtz describes the approach well in arguing that the Russians have made 'an exquisite strategic application of cyber power' to 'create "facts on the ground"' that creates a 'fait accompli while sidestepping NATO's deterrent.'[209] Since then, Ukraine has been subjected to a 'digital blitzkrieg' without abate, 'A hacker army has systematically undermined practically every sector of Ukraine: media, finance, transportation, military, politics, energy. Wave after wave of intrusions have deleted data, destroyed computers, and in some cases paralysed organisations most basic functions.'[210] The most significant example of such attacks to note is the BlackEnergy malware attack against Ukrainian power stations in December 2015 that cut the electricity to almost quarter of a million Ukrainians.[211] The BlackEnergy attack has since been surpassed by the Not-Petya ransomware – detailed earlier in the section on cybercrime– that escalated the test lab of Ukraine to one that incurred the first global-scale cyber collateral damage.

As a result of the inability to resolve the Russian intervention on any side, the stalemate in Ukraine has actually provided Russia with a more valuable use for such an ambiguous situation, 'using the country as a cyber-war testing ground – a laboratory for perfecting new forms of global online combat.'[212] Similar to the German use of the Spanish Civil War in the 1930s to hone war fighting techniques with their Condor Legion,[213] 'Where better to train an army of Kremlin hackers in digital combat than in the no-holds-barred atmosphere of a hot war inside the Kremlin's sphere of influence?'[214] The ability to be able to carry out such an extended campaign of experimentation unchallenged also highlights a dual purpose that is rightly established by Rid; they are also testing the edges of what the international community will tolerate. 'Russian hackers are testing out red lines, what they can get away with. . . . You push and see if you're pushed back. If not, you try the next step.'[215] The push back did not come, and that next step was not slow in coming.

The story of alleged Russian interference in the 2016 American presidential election is one that will continue for a long time to come. It has sparked a cascade of reflective analyses on the believed newfound weakness present in democracies; the turbulent administration led by Donald Trump has had countless notable casualties of resignations and removals as a result of the allegations. The most notable of these is the removal of James Comey as director of the FBI,[216] which as a case reveals the path towards a potential constitutional crisis in America itself. The highly controversial long-term inquiry led by Robert Mueller has since resulted, which is sure to present significant constitutional challenges if further evidence of Russian complicity is indeed found to have benefited from domestic collusion in any way.

The full timeline and details of the interference in the election is certainly beyond the art of the possible to cover in this work. Suffice to say that a long line of events stemming back to the breach of the Democratic National Committee in June 2015, from the exposure of presidential candidate Hilary Clinton's emails to the believed algorithmic exploitation of social media platforms such as Facebook and Twitter to disseminate fake news,[217] have all contributed to the questions that Mueller, at the time of writing, is pursuing. It was highly prescient that the *Oxford English Dictionary's* Word of the Year for 2016 was "post-truth," defined as 'relating to or denoting circumstances in which objective facts are less influential in shaping public opinions than appeals to emotion and personal belief.'[218]

A post-truth environment is one that is ripe for a Russia (disbelievers in objective truth itself, it should be remembered) that has long been honing numerous cyber tools to go on the offence with. Botnet armies on Twitter and exploitation of Facebook story feeds are strongly suspected of fuelling so-called "echo chambers" that 'help people self-segregate into like-minded filter bubbles'[219] of hatred and enmity, ensuring that public debate descends into a state of near emotive anarchy, where rivals are treated as enemies and intimidation of the free press prevails.[220] This has led to 'losing a sense of shared reality and the ability to communicate across social and sectarian lines.'[221] Companies such as Cambridge Analytica have been exposed[222] in their role in fine tuning algorithms, leading to the summons of Facebook CEO Marc Zuckerberg to Congress to provide answers in a public hearing in April 2018. This summons was precisely over the concern that even if companies like Cambridge Analytica have since gone out of business, been banned from platforms such as Facebook, and even deleted all data held, 'the information could have been used to perfect algorithms designed to understand the motivations and desires of millions'[223] that has led to the weaponisation of social media.

Details have since emerged from Facebook that believes a Russian-linked troll farm named the Internet Research Agency 'was responsible for at least 120 fake pages and 80,000 posts that were directly received by 29 (million) Americans. Through sharing and liking, the number grew to nearly 150 (million), about two-thirds of the potential electorate.'[224] American political scientist Kathleen Hall Jamieson has since published an extensive analysis of Russian impact on the 2016 election, specifically across three areas: press coverage, the presidential debates, and the last days of campaigning.[225] Jamieson concludes that 'Russia very likely delivered Trump's victory.'[226] While others take the view that social media was but one 'unwitting agent,'[227] Jamieson issues an outright criticism of those in charge of the numerous social media platforms in that they not only 'didn't anticipate the malign uses to which their systems could be put, but also failed to identify and thwart the illegal troll efforts to influence voters.'[228]

The unravelling of interference in the 2016 elections will continue; there is simply too much evidence on offer to invest much credence to President Trump's continued assertion that the investigation is no more than a "witch hunt." Instead, the growing body of opinion that 'Russia has been actively seeking to damage the fabric of American democracy'[229] will focus attention on to the insidious innovations in weaponising cyberspace as a key element to 'fight a war without actually being at war.'[230] This episode in particular is a clear example of Lucas Kello's state of *unpeace* prevailing,[231] whereby there is not a clear war at play, even a cold one, but an attack on the political process itself that seeks to undermine truth and trust, approaching Snyder's chilling warning that 'Post-truth is pre-fascism.'[232] Moore is also correct in his warning that the events of 2016 should be seen 'not as anomalies, but as models for what is coming next.'[233] The final word on the 2016 elections at this time must however lie with Vince Houghton, who simply states that 'This is going to be something that we'll study for a long time.'[234]

The final case to consider is a very brief one, the attempted assassination of Sergei Skripal in Salisbury, UK, in 2018 using Novichok nerve agent. The case of Skripal, a former Russian military intelligence officer who acted as a double agent for British intelligence and subsequently defected, is illustrative not in terms of any cyber component related to the case. Instead, it is highlighted here to demonstrate just how brazen Russia's attack on truth itself has become. In investigations involving both UK law enforcement as well as intelligence services, two Russian nationals were identified as the primary suspects – Alexander Petrov and Ruslan Borishov – whose movements during their time in the UK was extensively published through media outlets.[235]

The Russian media subsequently interviewed the two men, insisting they were simply tourists visiting Salisbury Cathedral,[236] before being exposed internationally as members of Russian military intelligence and special forces respectively. The unrelenting Russian denials of involvement in the face of strong international unity, including the imposition of fresh sanctions from the Trump administration,[237] are the most direct expression of Snyder's labelling of Putin's behaviour as *implausible deniability*.[238] This would be reinforced by strategic communications that 'used a highly decentralised approach in which all manner of players circulated any number of or alternative narratives with the aim of undermining the UK story.'[239] Having felt out the red lines that Rid warned of, it should be clear at this point that Russia clearly believes it can weather the international condemnation that comes without significant challenge or reprisal. A pattern of behaviour has been established that relies on implausible deniability, combined with an apparently new operational method that is actually an echo of past Russian strategic culture.

Much has been made of Russia's hybrid warfare techniques as a new operational method that is designed to pursue strategic goals without the overt deployment of military force, or to definitively provoke retaliatory measures such as NATO's Article V. This, however, is a simplistic notion of Russian methods, for the current behavioural pattern indeed carries strong echoes of a phrase that should be well known to those with an affinity for intelligence operations: active measures. 'Active measures are semi-covert or covert intelligence operations to shape an adversary's political decisions.'[240] Such measures have always had a cherished place in Russian operational method, stemming from their concept of *dezinformatsiya* at the beginning of the twentieth century. Indeed, as Allen and Moore outline, the Russian practice of pursuing foreign policy goals through subversion tangibly dates as far back as 1883 with the formation of the first czarist secret police, the Okhrana.[241] The best place to consult on the Russia affinity for active measures remains a 1998 CNN interview with former KGB Major General Oleg Kalugin, who described subversion as the heart and soul of Russian intelligence.

> Not intelligence collection, but subversion: active measures to weaken the West, to drive wedges in the Western community of alliances . . . to sow discord among allies, to weaken the United States in the eyes of the people of Europe, Asia, Africa, Latin America. . . . To make America more vulnerable to the anger and mistrust of other peoples.[242]

What is clear from this elucidation by Kalugin is that the assimilation of cyber means has been a logical progression of the traditional Russian practice of active measures as 'tactics of political warfare.'[243] Rid puts this into historical perspective well in his Congressional testimony; first, '*in the past 60 years, active measures became the norm.*' Second, '*in the past 20 years, aggressive Russian digital espionage campaigns became the norm.*' Third, '*in the past 2 years, Russian intelligence operators began to combine the two, hacking and leaking.*'[244] It is clear at this point that application of the new capabilities afforded by cyberspace as 'a primary theatre of Russia's asymmetrical activity'[245] has been pursued in a way that eluded Western categorisation entirely, allowing the term hybrid warfare to be mistakenly adopted instead of the more historically accurate active measures. Christopher Andrew best explains why this is so in his meta-history of intelligence in reminding readers that the KGB were far more successful than their American counterparts in retaining their operational secrets, especially those of active measures. 'No account of American policy in the Third World omits the role of CIA covert action. By contrast, KGB covert action ("active measures") passes almost unmentioned in most histories.'[246]

A Western lack of historical perspective is a contributing factor in not being able to understand and accurately categorise contemporary Russian activities as outlined above. By exploiting the promise of technology, Russia has been able to carry out a form of algorithmic exploitation against open Western societies and weaponise social media. By sowing doubt into every narrative, challenging every fact as unsubstantiated, and promiscuously levelling accusations of bias, Russia lies 'to assert power over truth itself.'[247] They have 'mastered the use of the global network as a force-projection platform and a space for cognitive manoeuvre.'[248] By asserting this now decisive tool of state power,[249] an 'information autocracy'[250] has emerged whereby Putin 'is president of his country and *king of reality.*'[251] The biggest victory that Putin could achieve would be to convince the liberal democracies that no such thing as objective truth exists; such a victory would be an important milestone in a competition against the West that to them never ended in 1991.

To conclude this first chapter, it is clear that although the technology of cyberspace carries significant conditioning realities and has benefited mightily from an infancy within an apolitical incubator, politics has returned in a big way indeed. The run of real-world events has presented both liberal democracies and authoritarian regimes alike with serious security problems, that have served to fuel the development of political visions for what the future of cyberspace should look like. All sides have been experimenting with how to use cyberspace, as has been detailed in this section immediately above; focus must now turn, however, to addressing the question of what solutions currently exist for the future development of cyberspace. Here is where attention turns to closer examination of the competing political visions being tabled for what the Internet of the future should look like.

Notes

1 NATO CCDCOE, *Resources: Cyber Definitions*. Available at https://ccdcoe.org/cyber-definitions.html
2 MoD, *Cyber Primer: Second Edition* (Swindon: DCDC, 2016), p. 7.
3 ITU quoted in Shmuel Even and David Siman-Tov, *Cyber Warfare: Concepts and Strategic Trends* (Tel Aviv: The Institute for National Security Studies, 2012), p. 10.
4 This is close to Blum's selection of three, the logical, physical, and geographical, but the author here argues for the combination of the physical and geographical, opting instead for the user as the core third area. Andrew Blum, *Tubes: A Journey to the Centre of the Internet* (New York: Harper Collins, 2012), p. 37.
5 The Internet Society, *Brief History of the Internet* (1997). Available at www.internetsociety.org/internet/history-internet/brief-history-internet/
6 Thomas Rid, *The Rise of the Machines: The Lost History of Cybernetics* (London: Scribe Publications, 2016). Although Rid's work is about more than simply cyberspace, his journey covers numerous elements of cyberspace's creation and application throughout the book.
7 Walter Isaacson, *The Innovators: How a Group of Inventors, Hackers, Geniuses, and Geeks Created the Digital Revolution* (London: Simon & Schuster, 2014), Ch. 7.
8 P. W. Singer and Allan Friedman, *Cybersecurity and Cyberwar: What Everyone Needs to Know* (New York: Oxford University Press, 2014), p. 55.
9 Isaacson (2014), p. 237.
10 Ibid (italics added).
11 Ibid, p. 239.
12 Paul Rosenzweig, *Cyber Warfare: How Conflicts in Cyberspace Are Challenging America and Changing the World* (Santa Barbara, CA: Praeger, 2013), p. 18.
13 The Internet Society (1997), p. 5.
14 Internetting and internetworking were early terms to articulate the concept of what packet switching would help to enable. Ibid, p. 5.

15 Tarnoff's 2016 article is useful in reminding all that an important origin of what is now cyberspace and the Internet was the US military. Ben Tarnoff, "How the Internet Was Invented", *The Guardian* (15 July 2016). Available at www. theguardian.com/technology/2016/jul/15/how-the-internet-was-invented-1976-arpa-kahn-cerf. Isaacson importantly contributed to this origin myth, by detailing that truth lies more in the middle in his recounting of how many disputed the nuclear survivability notion, while seniors at ARPA saw it not only as a core mission of the project, but also a key factor in the continuation of government funding of the emerging ARPANET. Isaacson (2014), pp. 246–248.

16 Singer and Friedman (2014), p. 72.

17 Myriam Dunn Cavelty and Elgin M. Brunner, "Introduction: Information, Power, and Security – an Outline of Debates and Implications", in Myriam Dunn Cavelty, Victor Mauer and Sani Felicia Krishna-Hensel (eds.), *Power and Security in the Information Age: Investigating the Roe of the State in Cyberspace* (Aldershot: Ashgate, 2007), pp. 8–9.

18 Jeremy Black, *The Power of Knowledge: How Information and Technology Made the Modern World* (London: Yale University Press, 2014), p. 15.

19 Tarnoff (2016).

20 The Internet Society (1997), p. 7.

21 There are numerous, deeper technical aspects of TCP/IP to outline. For current purposes, however, it is simply important to note the broad objectives of what TCP/IP serves and its success in achieving it. Microsoft's guidance online can more than cater to deeper technical explanation – Microsoft, *How TCP/IP Works*. Available at https://technet.microsoft.com/en-gb/library/cc786128(v=ws.10).aspx

22 Ibid.

23 The Internet Society (1997), p. 7.

24 Ibid, p. 9.

25 Blum (2012), pp. 95–96.

26 A point of relativity remains here, of course, in that access is determined by the scope of security precautions taken.

27 Rosenzweig (2013), p. 18.

28 Sarah Baranowski, *How Secure Are Root DNS Servers?* (Sans Institute, 2003), p. 1. Available at www.sans.org/reading-room/whitepapers/dns/security-issues-dns-1069www.sans.org/reading-room/whitepapers/dns/security-issues-dns-1069

29 Ibid, p. 2.

30 ICANN, *Factsheet: Root Server Attack on 6 February 2007* (1 March 2007), p. 6. Available at www.icann.org/en/system/files/files/factsheet-dns-attack-08mar07-en.pdf

31 Baranowski (2003), p. 2.

32 Vinton G. Cerf, "Foreword: Who Rules the Net?" in Adam Thierer and Clyde Wayne Crews Jr. (eds.), *Who Rules the Net? Internet Governance and Jurisdiction* (Washington, DC: The Cato Institute, 2003), p. x.

33 Singer and Friedman (2014), p. 73.

34 Known as DNS hijacking; Andy Greenberg, "Hacker Lexicon: What Is DNS Hijacking?" *Wired* (9 April 17). Available at www.wired.com/story/what-is-dns-hijacking/

35 The list of precise methods can run into a large compendium, as we are ultimately into the tactics of cyber attacks at this stage. These few examples, however, serve to illustrate some of the most persistent. Infoblox, *Whitepaper: Top*

Five DNS Security Attack Risks and How to Avoid Them, p. 4. Available at www.deepdivenetworking.com/files/infoblox-whitepaper-top5-dns-security-attack-risks-how-to-avoid-them_0.pdf

36 Ian Levy, *Active Cyber Defence – One Year On* (2018), 8.5, 8.6 and 8.7. Available at www.ncsc.gov.uk/information/active-cyber-defence-one-year
37 Rosenzweig (2013), p. 76.
38 ICANN (2007), p. 2.
39 Kim Davies, *There Are Not 13 Root Servers* (13 November 2007). Available at www.icann.org/news/blog/there-are-not-13-root-servers
40 Associated Press Security, "Servers Bounce Back from E-Attack", *Wired* (22 October 2002). Available at www.wired.com/2002/10/servers-bounce-back-from-e-attack/
41 Ibid.
42 ICANN (2007).
43 Nick Start, "How an Army of Vulnerable Gadgets Took Down the Internet Today", *The Verge* (21 October 16). Available at www.theverge.com/2016/10/21/13362354/dyn-dns-ddos-attack-cause-outage-status-explained
44 L. Carter, D. Burnett, S. Drew, G. Male, L. Hagadorn, D. Bartlett-McNeil and N. Irvine, *Submarine Cables and the Oceans: Connecting the World* (2009) UNEP-WCMC Biodiversity Series No. 31, p. 3.
45 Rishi Sunak, *Undersea Cables: Indispensable, Insecure* (London: Policy Exchange, 2017), p. 5.
46 Parag Khanna, *Connectography: Mapping the Future of Global Civilisation* (New York: Random House, 2016), p. 765.
47 "Sailing the Wired Seas", *The Economist* (10 March 2018), p. 11.
48 Blum (2012), p. 16.
49 Ibid, p. 22.
50 Frances Cairncross, *The Death of Distance: How the Communications Revolution Is Changing Our Lives* 2nd Ed. (London: Texere Publishing Limited, 2001), Ch. 1.
51 Luke Harding, "The Node Pole: Inside Facebook's Swedish Hub Near the Arctic Circle", *The Guardian* (25 September 2015). Available at www.theguardian.com/technology/2015/sep/25/facebook-datacentre-lulea-sweden-node-pole
52 Blum (2012), p. 22.
53 Cyber power is only power in as far as other actors are themselves networked. Danny Steed, "Cyber Power and Strategy – So What?" *Infinity Journal* (Spring 2011), 1, p. 23.
54 Sunak (2017), pp. 21–22.
55 Ibid, p. 12.
56 Ibid, p. 22.
57 Ewan MacAskill, Julian Border, Nick Hopkins, Nick Davies and James Ball, "GCHQ Taps Fibre-Optics Cables for Secret Access to World's Communications", *The Guardian* (21 June 2013). Available at www.theguardian.com/uk/2013/jun/21/gchq-cables-secret-world-communications-nsa
58 Luke Harding, *The Snowden Files: The Inside Story of the World's Most Wanted Man* (London: Vintage Books, 2014), Ch. 8.
59 MacAskill et al. (2013).
60 Blum (2012), Ch. 7.
61 Ibid, p. 388.

62   AWS Government, Education & Nonprofits Blog, *Announcing the New AWS Secret Region* (20 November 2017). Available at https://aws.amazon. com/blogs/publicsector/announcing-the-new-aws-secret-region/

63   Case Metz, "Amazon Wins Victory in Quest for Top Secret CIA Cloud", *Wired* (8 October 2013). Available at www.wired.com/2013/10/amazon-cia-2/

64   *Information Age*, "Getting Back to Business After Buncefield" (16 April 2006). Available at www.information-age.com/getting-back-to-business-after-buncefield-284331/

65   Sungard Availability Services, *Workplace Recovery Case Study: Northgate Information Solutions* (2014), p. 1. Available at www.sungardas.com/globalassets/_ multimedia/document-file/sungardas-northgate-information-solutions-case-study.pdf

66   Ibid, p. 2.

67   Bill Goodwin, "As Firms Count Cost of Oil Depot Blast, What Are the Disaster Recovery Lessons?" *Computer Weekly Blog* (January 2006). Available at www. computerweekly.com/feature/As-firms-count-cost-of-oil-depot-blast-what-are-the-disaster-recovery-lessons

68   Tim Webb, "Firms Still Missing Data Lost in Buncefield Oil Depot Blaze", *The Independent* (1 January 2006). Available at www.independent.co.uk/news/business/news/firms-still-missing-data-lost-in-buncefield-oil-depot-blaze-335867.html

69   DHI News Team, "Hemel Explosion Hits Northgate Hospital Customers" (14 December 2005). Available at www.digitalhealth.net/2005/12/hemel-explosion-hits-northgate-hospital-customers/

70   Rosenzweig (2013), p. 202.

71   Edward Lucas, *Cyberphobia: Identity, Trust, Security and the Internet* (London: Bloomsbury, 2016), p. 532.

72   Panayotis A. Yannakogeorgos, "Internet Governance and National Security", *Strategic Studies Quarterly* (Fall 2012), p. 103.

73   Jacob Brogan, "What Is Internet Governance?" *Slate* (1 November 2016). Available at www.slate.com/articles/technology/future_tense/2016/11/what_exactly_ is_internet_governance.html

74   2005 World Summit on the Information Society quoted in Jonathan Masters, *What Is Internet Governance?* Council on Foreign Relations (23 April 2014). Available at www.cfr.org/backgrounder/what-internet-governance

75   Klimburg (2017), pp. 88–89.

76   Cerf (2003), p. x.

77   Klimburg (2017), p. 89.

78   Ibid, p. 94.

79   Singer and Friedman (2014), p. 85.

80   Yannakogeorgos (Fall 2012), p. 113.

81   Singer and Friedman (2014), p. 85.

82   Klimburg (2017), p. 95.

83   Singer and Friedman (2014), p. 87.

84   The Internet Society, *Our Mission*. Available at www.internetsociety.org/mission/

85   Klimburg (2017), p. 98.

86   Clyde Wayne Crews Jr. And Adam Thierer, "Introduction: Who Rules the Net?" in Thierer and Crews Jr. (2003), p. xx.

87   Isaacson is necessary reading to temper many public myths around the growth of cyberspace, in this case including the chronology of American legislation that opened the gates for a public rollout of the Internet. Isaacson (2014), p. 402.

88 ICANN, *General ICANN Factsheet* (November 2013). Available at www. icann.org/resources/pages/factsheets-2012-02-25-en

89 ICANN, *The IANA Functions* (December 2015). Available at www.icann.org/ en/system/files/files/iana-functions-18dec15-en.pdf

90 ICANN, *What Does ICANN Do?* Available at www.icann.org/resources/ pages/welcome-2012-02-25-en

91 Klimburg (2017), p. 103.

92 ICANN, *How Does ICANN Work?* Available at www.icann.org/resources/ pages/welcome-2012-02-25-en

93 Klimburg (2017), p. 102.

94 Singer and Friedman (2014), p. 85.

95 Lucas (2016), p. 533.

96 Klimburg (2017), p. 105.

97 Kal Raustiala, "An Internet Whole and Free: Why Washington Was Right to Give Up Control", *Foreign Affairs* (March–April 2017), 96:2, pp. 142–143.

98 Ibid, p. 141.

99 Isaacson (2014), pp. 246–248.

100 Michael Belfiore, *The Department of Mad Scientists: How DARPA Is Remaking Our World, from the Internet to Artificial Limbs* (London: Harper Collins eBooks, 2010), Ch. 3.

101 Isaacson (2014), Ch. 10 skilfully pairs the, heretofore, separate developments of cyberspace and the Personal Computer.

102 Ibid, p. 308.

103 Raustiala (2017), p. 143.

104 James A. Lewis, "Sovereignty and the Role of the Government in Cyberspace", *Brown Journal of World Affairs* (Spring–Summer 2010), XVI:II, p. 58.

105 "Tim Cook, Privacy Martyr?" *The Economist* (20 February 2016). Available at www.economist.com/business/2016/02/20/tim-cook-privacy-martyr

106 John Cassidy, "Lessons from Apple vs the FBI", *The New Yorker* (29 March 2016). Available at www.newyorker.com/news/john-cassidy/lessons-from-apple-versus-the-f-b-i

107 The White House, *Remarks by President Obama and Prime Minister Cameron of the United Kingdom in Joint Press Conference* (16 January 2015). Available at https://obamawhitehouse.archives.gov/the-press-office/2015/01/16/remarks-president-obama-and-prime-minister-cameron-united-kingdom-joint-

108 This will be dealt with in greater detail in the next section below.

109 Tony Romm, "Facebook's Zuckerberg Just Survived 10 Hours of Questioning by Congress", *The Washington Post* (11 April 2018). Available at www. washingtonpost.com/news/the-switch/wp/2018/04/11/zuckerberg-facebook-hearing-congress-house-testimony/?utm_term=.3ff93cbec654

110 Sheer Frenkel, Nicholas Confessore, Cecilia Kang, Matthew Rosenberg and Jack Nicas, "Delay, Deny and Deflect: How Facebook's Leaders Fought Through Crisis", *The New York Times* (14 November 2018). Available at www.nytimes.com/2018/11/14/technology/facebook-data-russia-election-racism.html

111 Consisting of Argentine, Belgium, Brazil, Canada, France, Ireland, Latvia, Singapore, and the UK.

112 "MPs Fury Over Mark Zuckerberg 'no show'", *BBC News* (27 November 2018). Available at www.bbc.com/news/technology-46357359

113 Walden quoted in Tony Romm (11 April 2018).

114 Henry Kissinger, *World Order: Reflections on the Characters of Nations and the Course of History* (London: Penguin Books, 2015), p. 565.

115 A superbly comprehensive start would lie, however, with Melvyn P. Leffler and Odd Arne Westad (ed.), *The Cambridge History of the Cold War Vol. I–III* (Cambridge: Cambridge University Press, 2010).
116 Philip Bobbitt, *The Shield of Achilles: War, Peace and the Course of History* (London: Penguin Books, 2002), Part One.
117 Francis Fukuyama, *The End of History and the Last Man* (New York: The Free Press, 1992).
118 Ibid, p. xiii.
119 Barry Buzan, "Economic Structure and International Security: The Limits of the Liberal Case", in Barry Buzan and Lene Hansen (eds.), *International Security Volume II: The Transition to the Post-Cold War Security Agenda* (Los Angeles, CA: Sage Publications Ltd., 2007), p. 2.
120 G. John Ikenberry, "The Restructuring of the International System After the Cold War", in Melvyn P. Leffler and Odd Arne Westad (eds.), *The Cambridge History of the Cold War Volume III: Endings* (Cambridge: Cambridge University Press, 2010), p. 547.
121 The list on the British Empire is, much like that of the Second World War, near endless. A sufficient reading of the following would, however, provide enough of an understanding of the range of disputes about Britain's relative decline: Piers Brendon, *The Decline and Fall of the British Empire, 1781–1997* (New York: Alfred A. Knopf, 2008); John Darwin, *The Empire Project: The Rise and Fall of the British World System, 1830–1970* (Cambridge: Cambridge University Press, 2009); and Paul Kennedy, *The Rise and Fall of the Great Powers: Economic Change and Military Conflict from 1500 to 2000* (New York: Vintage Books, 1987), Ch. 4.
122 Bacevich is correct in stating by the early 1990s that America was 'unarguably the greatest power in all recorded history.' Andrew J. Bacevich, *American Empire: The Realities and Consequences of US Diplomacy* (Cambridge, MA: Harvard University Press, 2004), p. 242.
123 Ikenberry in Leffler and Westad (2010), p. 556.
124 Robert Kagan, *The World America Made* (New York: Alfred A. Knopf, 2012), Ch. 5.
125 Andrew Krepinevich, *7 Deadly Scenarios: A Military Futurist Explores War in the 21st Century* (New York: Bantam Books, 2009), p. 317.
126 Niall Ferguson, *Colossus: The Rise and Fall of the American Empire* (New York: Penguin Books, 2009), p. 709.
127 Ibid, p. 734.
128 Usefully labelled by Burke in the title to his history of the period. Jason Burke, *The 9/11 Wars* (London: Penguin Books, 2012).
129 Like many of the political watershed moments mentioned in this book, the literature on the 2008 crash is substantial. A reading of Adam Tooze's *Crashed: How a Decade of Financial Crises Changed the World* (London: Allan Lane, 2018) is a more than worthy account carrying historical perspective.
130 For a recent and most worthy account of the Marshall Plan, see Benn Steil, *The Marshall Plan: Dawn of the Cold War* (London: Simon & Schuster, 2018).
131 Zbigniew Brzezinski, *Strategic Vision: America and the Crisis of Global Power* (New York: Basic Books, 2012) p. 32.
132 Raustiala (March–April 2017), p. 142.
133 Available at www.symantec.com/security-center/threat-report
134 Available at https://ssl.www8.hp.com/ww/en/secure/pdf/4aa6-3786enw.pdf

135 Available at https://news.hpe.com/state-of-security-operations-2017/
136 Available at www.nttsecurity.com/en-uk/landing-pages/2018-gtir
137 Available at www.microsoft.com/en-gb/security/intelligence-report
138 HPE Security Research, *Cyber Risk Report* (2016), p. 90.
139 NTT Group, *Global Threat Intelligence Report* (2016), p. 5.
140 Symantec, *Internet Security Threat Report* (April 2016), 21, p. 5.
141 Kaspersky KSN Report, *Ransomware in 2014–2016* (June 2016), p. 2. Available at https://securelist.com/pc-ransomware-in-2014-2016/75145/
142 DCMS, *Cyber Security Breaches Survey* (2018). Available at www.gov.uk/government/statistics/cyber-security-breaches-survey-2018
143 Davey Winder, "How Organised Is Organised Cybercrime?" *Raconteur. Special Report: Cyber-Risk & Resilience* (17 December 2017), p. 8. Available at www.raconteur.net/risk-management/how-organised-is-organised-cybercrime
144 McAfee, *Economic Impact of Cybercrime – No Slowing Down* (February 2018), p. 4. Available at www.mcafee.com/enterprise/en-us/solutions/lp/economics-cybercrime.html
145 Ibid, p. 22.
146 HMG, *The UK Cyber Security Strategy: Protecting and Promoting the UK in a Digital World* (2011), p. 8. Available at www.gov.uk/government/publications/cyber-security-strategy
147 Rosenzweig (2013), Ch. 3.
148 Paulo Shakarian, Jana Shakarian and Andrew Ruef, *Introduction to Cyber-Warfare: A Multidisciplinary Approach* (Waltham, MA: Syngress, 2013), p. 300.
149 There are so many instances of suspected breaches in this regard to make a specific citation near futile; a cursory Google search will take readers to several suspected instances.
150 Siobhan Gorman, "Electricity Grid in the US Penetrated by Spies", *The Wall Street Journal* (8 April 2009). Available at www.wsj.com/articles/SB123914805204099085
151 Ben Elgin, Dune Lawrence and Michael Riley, "Coke Gets Hacked and Doesn't Tell Anyone", *Bloomberg* (4 November 2012). Available at www.bloomberg.com/news/articles/2012-11-04/coke-hacked-and-doesn-t-tell
152 Siobhan Gorman, "China Hackers Hit US Chamber", *The Wall Street Journal* (21 December 2011). Available at www.wsj.com/articles/SB10001424052970204058404577110541568535300
153 Kim Zetter, "Report: Hackers Seized Control of Computers in NASA's Jet Propulsion Lab", *Wired* (3 January 2012). Available at www.wired.com/2012/03/jet-propulsion-lab-hacked/
154 For a comprehensive report see the Committee on Oversight and Government Reform, US House of Representatives, 114th Congress, *The OPM Data Breach: How the Government Jeopardized our National Security for More Than a Generation* (7 October 2016). Available at https://oversight.house.gov/wp-content/uploads/2016/09/The-OPM-Data-Breach-How-the-Government-Jeopardized-Our-National-Security-for-More-than-a-Generation.pdf
155 Edmund Brumaghin, Ross Gibb, Warren Mercer, Matthew Molyett and Craig Williams, "CCleanup: A Vast Number of Machines at Risk", *Cisco Talos* (18 September 2017). Available at https://blog.talosintelligence.com/2017/09/avast-distributes-malware.html
156 Ellan Nakashima and Paul Sonne, "China Hacked a Navy Contractor and Secured a Trove of Highly Sensitive Data on Submarine Warfare", *The Washington Post*

(8 June 2018). Available at www.washingtonpost.com/world/national-security/ china-hacked-a-navy-contractor-and-secured-a-trove-of-highly-sensitive-data-on-submarine-warfare/2018/06/08/6cc396fa-68e6-11e8-bea7-c8eb28bc52b1_ story.html?noredirect=on&utm_term=.b579d3932ba1

157 Jordan Robertson and Michael Riley, "The Big Hack: How China Used a Tiny Chip to Infiltrate US Companies", *Bloomberg Businessweek* (4 October 2018). Available at www.bloomberg.com/news/features/2018-10-04/the-big-hack-how-china-used-a-tiny-chip-to-infiltrate-america-s-top-companies

158 Janko Roettgers, "Apple Denies Bloomberg's China Hack Report in Letter to Congress", *Variety* (8 October 2018). Available at https://variety. com/2018/digital/news/apple-denies-bloombergs-china-hack-report-in-letter-to-congress-1202972155/

159 NCSC, *ZTE: NCSC Advice to Select Telecommunications Operators with National Security Concerns* (16 April 2018). Available at www.ncsc.gov.uk/ news/zte-ncsc-advice-select-telecommunications-operators-national-security-concerns-0

160 Remarks by President Obama and President Xi of the People's Republic of China in a Joint Press Conference (25 October 2015). Available at https://obamawhitehouse.archives.gov/the-press-office/2015/09/25/remarks-president-obama-and-president-xi-peoples-republic-china-joint

161 Joseph Menn and Joe Finkle, "Chinese Economic Cyber-Espionage Plummets in US: Experts", *Reuters* (21 June 2016). Available at www.reuters.com/article/ us-cyber-spying-china/chinese-economic-cyber-espionage-plummets-in-u-s-experts-idUSKCN0Z700D

162 Scott W. Harold, "The US-China Cyber Agreement: A Good First Step", *The RAND Blog* (1 August 2016). Available at www.rand.org/blog/2016/08/the-us-china-cyber-agreement-a-good-first-step.html

163 Andy Greenberg, "China Tests the Limits of Its US Hacking Truce", *Wired* (31 October 2017). Available at www.wired.com/story/china-tests-limits-of-us-hacking-truce/

164 David E. Sanger and Steven Lee Myers, "After a Hiatus, China Accelerates Cyberspying Efforts to Obtain US Technology", *The New York Times* (29 November 2018). Available at www.nytimes.com/2018/11/29/us/politics/china-trump-cyberespionage.html

165 Singer and Friedman (2014), p. 233.

166 Ibid, p. 234.

167 Remarks by the President at the Cybersecurity and Consumer Protection Summit (13 February 2015). Available at https://obamawhitehouse.archives.gov/ the-press-office/2015/02/13/remarks-president-cybersecurity-and-consumer-protection-summit

168 Klimburg (2017), p. 316.

169 Lucas Kello, *The Virtual Weapon and International Order* (London: Yale University Press, 2017), p. 4.

170 Howard W. French, *Everything Under the Heavens: How the Past Helps Shapes China's Push for Global Power* (New York: Alfred A. Knopf, 2017), p. 660.

171 Harden Tibbs, *The Global Cyber Game: The Defence Academy Cyber Inquiry Report* (London: MoD, 2013), p. 107.

172 Fergus Hanson, *Internet Wars: The Struggle for Power in the Twenty-First Century* (Haberfield, NSW: Longueville Media, 2015), p. 15.

173 Philip N. Howard, Alden Duffy, Deen Freelon, Muzammil Hussain, Will Mari and Marwa Muzaid, *Opening Closed Regimes: What Was the Role of Social Media During the Arab Spring?* (January 2011) Project on Information Technology and Political Islam, Working Paper, p. 23.
174 Taylor Dewey, Julianne Kaden, Miriam Marks, Shun Matsushima and Beijing Zhu, *The Impact of Social Media on Social Unrest in the Arab Spring* (2012), p. viii. Available at https://publicpolicy.stanford.edu/publications/impact-social-media-social-unrest-arab-spring
175 Ibid, p. 50.
176 David Patrikarakos, *War in 140 Characters: How Social Media Is Reshaping Conflict in the Twenty-First Century* (New York: Basic Books, 2017), p. 9.
177 Richard A. Lindsey, "What the Arab Spring Tells Us About the Future of Social Media in Revolutionary Movements", *Small Wars Journal* (2013). Available at http://smallwarsjournal.com/jrnl/art/what-the-arab-spring-tells-us-about-the-future-of-social-media-in-revolutionary-movements
178 Planning Outline for the Construction of a Social Credit System (2014-2020) Posted on 14 June 2014 updated on 25 April, 2015, State Council Notice concerning Issuance of the Planning Outline for the Construction of a Social Credit System (2014–2020) GF No. (2014), 21. Available at https://chinacopyrightandmedia.wordpress.com/2014/06/14/planning-outline-for-the-construction-of-a-social-credit-system-2014–2020/
179 Paul Mozur, "Inside China's Dystopian Dreams: A.I., Shame and Lots of Cameras", *The New York Times* (8 July 2018). Available at www.nytimes.com/2018/07/08/business/china-surveillance-technology.html
180 Privacy International Topics Cover a Wide Range of Data Collection, Protection, and Surveillance Topics. Available at https://privacyinternational.org/topics
181 State Council Notice (2014).
182 Second guessing such a list would be a long venture, but one could immediately suspect items such as alcohol, books seen as defamatory, revealing clothing, Western media products like music, movies, and video games, non-indigenously built cars comprising basic elements.
183 The detailing of these categories is sourced from Rachel Botsman, *Who Can You Trust: How Technology Brought Us Together and Why It Might Drive Us Apart* (New York: Public Affairs, 2017), pp. 269–272.
184 Ibid, p. 272.
185 Charles Rollet, "The Odd Reality of Life Under China's All-Seeing Credit Score System", *Wired* (5 June 2018). Available at www.wired.co.uk/article/china-social-credit
186 Oliver Moody, "Big Brother Is Watching Them. And We're Next", *The Times* (31 March 2018), p. 33.
187 Ibid.
188 Cathy O'Neill, *Weapons of Math Destruction: How Big Data Increases Inequality and Threatens Democracy* (London: Penguin Books, 2017).
189 Rachel Botsman, "Big Data Meets Big Brother as China Moves to Rate Its Citizens", *Wired* (21 October 2017). Available at https:www.wired.co.uk/article/chinese-government-social-credit-score-privacy-invasion
190 Botsman (2017), p. 283.
191 Moody (2018), p. 33.
192 This being the title of *The Economist* article in "The Future of War" Special Report. *The Economist* (27 January– 2 February 2018), p. 7.

193 George Kennan, *The Charge in the Soviet Union (Kennan) to the Secretary of State* (22 February 1949), commonly known as "Kennan's Long Telegram" (italics added). Available at https://nsarchive2.gwu.edu//coldwar/documents/episode-1/kennan.htm

194 The number of incidents whereby NATO nations have scrambled interceptions is far too numerous to cover, yet even this outdated source illustrates volume well. Roland Oliphant and Darren Soulsby, "Mapped: Just How Many Incursions into NATO Airspace Has Russian Military Made?" *The Telegraph* (15 March 2015). Available at www.telegraph.co.uk/news/worldnews/europe/russia/11609783/Mapped-Just-how-many-incursions-into-Nato-airspace-has-Russian-military-made.html

195 Mariano Castillo and Lindsay Isaac, "Sweden Confirms Foreign Sub in Its Waters", *CNN International* (14 November 2014). Available at https://edition.cnn.com/2014/11/14/world/europe/sweden-russia-submarine-mystery/index.html

196 One can cite the assassination of Alexander Litvinenko in London, with the UK Parliamentary Inquiry concluding it was a state-sanctioned mission. Sir Robert Owen (Chair), *The Litvinenko Inquiry* (2016). Available at www.gov.uk/government/publications/the-litvinenko-inquiry-report-into-the-death-of-alexander-litvinenko. But the 2018 attempted assassination of Sergei Skripal in the UK is also a highly pertinent example that will be addressed later.

197 Jonathan Marcus, "Russia vs the West: Is This a New Cold War?" *BBC News* (1 April 2018). Available at www.bbc.com/news/world-europe-43581449

198 Kennan (1949).

199 Vladimir Putin has been famously quoted in his 2005 speech as referring to the breakup of the Soviet Union as the 'greatest geopolitical catastrophe of the century,' although there remain some disagreements as to the translations offered. Katie Sanders, "Did Vladimir Putin Call the Breakup of the USSR 'the greatest geopolitical tragedy of the 20th century?'" *Politifact* (6 March 2014). Available at www.politifact.com/punditfact/statements/2014/mar/06/john-bolton/did-vladimir-putin-call-breakup-ussr-greatest-geop/

200 Arkady Ostrovsky, *The Invention of Russia: The Rise of Putin and the Age of Fake News* (New York: Penguin Books, 2017), p. 41.

201 Fred Kaplan, "The Info Wars to Come", *Slate* (8 September 2017). Available at https://slate.com/news-and-politics/2017/09/russia-is-weaponizing-social-media.html

202 Giles is right to label Georgia under 'The Old Information War', Keir Giles, *Russia's "New" Tools for Confronting the West: Continuity and Innovation in Moscow's Exercise of Power* (London: Chatham House, March 2016), Ch. 4. Available at www.chathamhouse.org/publication/russias-new-tools-confronting-west#; but this author's own effort is offered for further examination on the case: Danny Steed, "The Strategic Implications of Cyber Warfare", in James Andrew Green (ed.), *Cyber Warfare: A Multidisciplinary Analysis* (Abingdon: Routledge, 2015).

203 Vitaly Shevchenko, "'Little green men' or 'Russian invaders'?" *BBC News* (11 March 2014). Available at www.bbc.com/news/world-europe-26532154

204 Andy Greenberg, "How an Entire Nation Became Russia's Test Lab for Cyberwar", *Wired* (20 June 2017). Available at www.wired.com/story/russian-hackers-attack-ukraine/

205 Tom Parfitt, "Operation Troy: The Blueprint for Spreading Chaos in Ukraine", *The Times* (2 April 2018), p. 8.
206 Giles (2016), p. 7.
207 Bob Seely and Alya Sandra, "The Toolkit for Kremlin's New Warfare", *The Times* (2 April 2018), p. 9.
208 Giles (2016), p. 32.
209 James J. Wirtz, "Cyber War and Strategic Culture: The Russian Integration of Cyber Power into Grand Strategy", in Kenneth Geers (ed.), *Cyber War in Perspective: Russian Aggression Against Ukraine* (Tallinn: NATO CCDCOE, 2015), p. 36.
210 Greenberg (2017).
211 Best covered by ICS-CERT, Alert (IR-Alert-H-16–056–01) *Cyber-Attack Against Ukrainian Critical Infrastructure* (25 February 2016). Available at https://ics-cert.us-cert.gov/alerts/IR-ALERT-H-16-056-01
212 Greenberg (2017).
213 For a detailed consideration of German activities, see Ian Westwell, *Condor Legion: The Wehrmacht's Training Ground* (London: Ian Allan Publishing, 2004).
214 Greenberg (2017).
215 Thomas Rid quoted in ibid.
216 Comey has detailed his experience and perspective since. James Comey, *A Higher Loyalty: Truth, Lies, and Leadership* (London: Macmillan, 2018).
217 "2016 Presidential Election Hacking Fast Facts", *CNN Library* (18 October 2018). Available at https://edition.cnn.com/2016/12/26/us/2016-presidential-campaign-hacking-fast-facts/index.html
218 *Oxford English Dictionary Word of the Year 2016.* Available at https://en.oxford dictionaries.com/word-of-the-year/word-of-the-year-2016
219 Roger McNamee, "How to Fix Facebook – Before It Fixes Us", *Washington Monthly* (January–March 2018). Available at https://washingtonmonthly.com/magazine/january-february-march-2018/how-to-fix-facebook-before-it-fixes-us/
220 Steven Levitsky and Daniel Ziblatt, *How Democracies Die* (New York: Crown Publishers, 2018), p. 10.
221 Michiko Kakutani, *The Death of Truth: Notes on Falsehood in the Age of Trump* (New York: Tim Duggan Books, 2018), p. 10.
222 Christopher Wylie whistle blew to the UK-based newspaper *The Observer.* Christopher Wylie, "Why I Broke Facebook Data Story – and What Should Happen Now", *The Observer* (8 April 2018).
223 Murad Ahmed, Hannah Kuchler and Matthew Garrahan, "How Digital Footprints Paved Way to Weaponising Social Media", *The Financial Times* (18 March 2018). Available at www.ft.com/content/f369e670-2ac3-11e8-9b4b-bc4b9f08f381
224 "My Truth Against Yours", "The Future of War" Special Report. *The Economist* (27 January–2 February 2018), p. 7.
225 Kathleen Hall Jamieson, *Cyber-War: How Russian Hackers and Trolls Helped Elect a President, What We Don't, Can't, and Do Know* (New York: Oxford University Press, 2018).
226 Jane Meyer, "How Russia Helped Swing the Election for Trump", *The New Yorker* (1 October 2018). Available at www.newyorker.com/magazine/2018/10/01/how-russia-helped-to-swing-the-election-for-trump

227 Thomas Rid referred specifically to Twitter in this regard. Thomas Rid, "Dis-information: A Primer in Russian Active Measures and Influence Campaigns", Testimony to the 150th Congress (30 March 2017), Hearings before the Select Committee on Intelligence, Unites States Senate, p. 5. Available at www.intel ligence.senate.gov/sites/default/files/documents/os-trid-033017.pdf
228 Jamieson (2018), p. 218.
229 Michael V. Hayden, *The Assault on Intelligence: American National Security in an Age of Lies* (New York: Penguin Books, 2018), p. 15.
230 Jarno Limnell, "The Exploitation of Cyber Domain as Part of Warfare: Russo-Ukrainian War", *International Journal of Cyber-Security and Digital Foren-sics* (2015), 4:4, p. 531.
231 Kello (2017), p. 249.
232 Timothy Snyder, *On Tyranny: Twenty Lessons from the Twentieth Century* (New York: Tim Duggan Books, 2017), p. 74.
233 Martin Moore, *Democracy Hacked: Political Turmoil and Information War-fare in the Digital Age* (London: Oneworld Publications Ltd., 2018), p. xii.
234 Vince Houghton quoted in Kaveh Waddell, "Does Russia's Election Hacking Signal a New Era in Espionage?" *The Atlantic* (15 December 2016). Available at www.theatlantic.com/technology/archive/2016/12/russias-election-meddling-was-an-intelligence-coup/510743/
235 "Russian Spy: What Happened to Sergei and Yulia Skripal?" *BBC News* (27 September 2018). Available at www.bbc.com/news/uk-43643025
236 Andrew Roth and Vikran Dodd, "Salisbury Poisoning Suspect Identified as Russian Colonel", *The Guardian* (26 September 2018). Available at www.theguardian.com/world/2018/sep/26/salisbury-poisoning-suspect-is-russian-colonel-reports
237 Rozina Sabur and Harriet Alexander, "US Imposes Sanctions on Russia Over Salisbury Poisoning of Skripals", *The Telegraph* (8 August 2018). Avail-able at www.telegraph.co.uk/news/2018/08/08/us-imposes-sanctions-russia-salisbury-spy-poisoning/
238 Timothy Snyder, *The Road to Unfreedom: Russia, Europe, America* (New York: Tim Duggan Books, 2018), p. 307.
239 Mark Urban, *The Skripal Files: The Life and Near Death of a Russian Spy* (London: Henry Holt & Company, 2018), p. 429.
240 Thomas Rid Congressional Testimony (2017), p. 1.
241 T. S. Allen and A. J. Moore, "Victory Without Casualties: Russia's Information Operations", *Parameters* (Spring 2018), 48:1, p. 61.
242 "An Interview with Retired KGB Maj. Gen. Oleg Kalugin", *CNN* (Janu-ary 1998). Available at https://web.archive.org/web/20070206020316/www.cnn.com/SPECIALS/cold.war/episodes/21/interviews/kalugin/
243 Brad D. Williams, "How Russia Adapted KGB 'active measures' to Cyber Operations, Part I", *Fifth Domain* (19 March 2017). Available at www.fifth domain.com/home/2017/03/19/how-russia-adapted-kgb-active-measures-to-cyber-operations-part-i/
244 Thomas Rid Congressional Testimony (2017), pp. 2–3 (italics original).
245 Pasi Eronen, "Russian Hybrid Warfare: How to Confront a New Challenge to the West", *Foundation for Defence of Democracies* (June 2016), p. 6. Available at www.fdd.org/analysis/2016/06/01/russian-hybrid-warfare-how-to-confront-a-new-challenge-to-the-west/

246 Christopher Andrew, *The Secret World: A History of Intelligence* (London: Allen Lane, 2018), p. 8.
247 Kakutani (2018), p. 121.
248 Allen and Moore (2018), p. 69.
249 Ibid, p. 59.
250 Daniel Treisman (Ed.), *The New Autocracy: Information, Politics, and Policy in Putin's Russia* (Washington, DC: The Brookings Institution, 2018), p. 44.
251 Kakutani (2018), p. 122 (italic added).

2 What solutions exist for the future of cyberspace?

2.1 Introduction

The previous chapter sought to achieve an extended pairing of the technical realities of cyberspace with political concerns, in order to establish what circumstances have led to the stage of cyber *in*-security that typifies the current era. Instead of relying on hyperbole and grandiose hypotheses that typify most journalism and even much scholarship, this work has sought to match empirical evidence of the types of behaviours and actions we have seen so far with the historical context of the politics within and amongst which those behaviours and actions have grown. Doing so has enabled a key reality and two key arguments of this work to emerge: (1) *that cyberspace has so far enjoyed a honeymoon period of apolitical governance thanks to the victory of the liberal order in the Cold War* and (2) *due to the significant and persistent insecurities that the Internet has brought to today's world, politics is now fully committed to reasserting its sovereign authority on this space.*

With these arguments in place, it is now necessary to turn to the next research question, what solutions lie ahead? The answer to this question is a far more political story, exploring in detail the political divergence mentioned in Chapter 1. Despite this, however, there will certainly be the evolution of technological realities to consider, as well as how they might – for we are certainly in the realm of speculation in this regard – shape the contours of what is politically feasible. Before this exploration takes place, however, a brief introductory segment is required on a core political concept that animates the essence of the dispute in future approaches to the place of political authority in cyberspace: sovereignty.

Sovereignty lies at the heart of the nation-state system, originating from the Peace of Westphalia that ended the Thirty Years War in 1648 which, through the signing of various treaties to end that war across Europe, established the norm against interference in the domestic affairs of other political entities. Sovereignty in this view 'refers to the supreme authority of the prince or king or, applied to modern international law, the State.'[1] The possession of sovereign status 'confers rights on two distinct planes or spheres: the domestic sphere and the international sphere.'[2] Domestically, sovereign status is intended to guarantee non-interference in the internal affairs of a political unit, be it a principality, kingdom, or modern state unit. Internationally, regardless of the size of the political community in question, sovereign actors are seen as equal among each other in both status and rights.

At this point, there also needs to be recognition of the limitations that exist regarding sovereignty, for it is not an absolute concept. The first limitation that exists is naturally the extent of one sovereign's authority in relation to others, which has always been based on geographic boundaries; there is an acknowledgement of a 'geographical limitation to the legitimate use of power, as embodied in the concepts of territorial integrity and sanctity of borders.'[3] Additionally, in the modern era of codified international law, sovereignty is limited by certain principles, including actions determined by the UN Security Council, the established Laws of Armed Conflict, and fundamental human rights.[4] Further, other areas are agreed to be beyond the assertion of state sovereignty; these include the international waters of the high seas, non-exclusive sovereignty in Antarctica, the seabed, and extraterrestrial areas such as the moon. 'These are areas where no sovereign exercises power, but where all sovereigns share power, based on agreement.'[5]

So far, these legal assertions of the meaning of sovereignty make it appear a very clinical and clean concept, when in fact it is anything but. Powers and Jablonski are quite right to state that it is 'Never absolute, always contested, conceptions of sovereignty have evolved over time as a means of enhancing legitimacy and easing social tensions.'[6] Indeed, when one looks closely at global events, one will find frequent cases of the challenge to question sovereign status, and the continuing activities in the South China Sea are a clear demonstration of this away from cyberspace. China has in recent years embarked on a programme of constructing artificial islands across the South China Sea in an attempt to assert its sovereign status – and with it exclusive rights to sources of fishing and minerals – over areas that have to date remained ruled by none under the provisions of the UN Conventions on the Laws of the Sea. This has precipitated a response programme, led primarily by the US Navy, to assert "Freedom of Navigation" exercises throughout the region as a demonstration that this attempt to extend sovereign authority is not recognised.[7]

What this brief mention of the continuing disputes over sovereign status in the South China Sea is intended to do is reveal, on one front, the reality of sovereignty as a constantly challenged concept in the day-to-day realities of political actions and discourse. Cyberspace represents another core front in the challenge for asserting one's sovereign authority; with the return of politics to cyberspace established in Chapter 1, it is now time to examine the arguments for establishing sovereign authority over this space.

2.2 Cyber Sovereignty

> We should respect the right of individual countries to independently choose their own path of cyber development, model of cyber regulation and Internet public policies, and participate in international cyberspace governance on an equal footing. No country should pursue cyber hegemony, interfere in other countries' internal affairs, or engage in, connive at or support cyber activities that undermine other countries' national security.[8]

Xi Jinping's remarks to the Second World Internet Conference at Wuzhen in 2015 very effectively encapsulate the Chinese view of what Cyber Sovereignty should entail. This concept differs from cyber security for quite a simple distinction – whereas cyber security as a term concerns protecting the underlying infrastructure and processes connecting to the Internet itself, Cyber Sovereignty 'focuses on the information and content provided by the Internet.'[9] This core distinction very much reveals the desire to secure internal stability above all other concerns. Furthermore, Klimburg asserts that it is a shift in focus, that 'China has abandoned its time-honoured maxim of "hiding one's strength and biding one's time" and begun to assert cyber power more proactively.'[10] This proactivity and emergence of a clear stand on Cyber Sovereignty has been in line with the broader trends of China's emerging foreign policy[11] and is arguably reflective of Corera's observation that China may be motivated by the fear that Internet freedom may be nothing more than the 'freedom to be exploited and spied on by the US and its companies.'[12]

Cyber Sovereignty has emerged, therefore, as the primary challenge to the Western liberal view of Internet Freedom and multi-stakeholderism as an alternative model, a clear demonstration that 'passive sovereignty is evolving into a more active assertion of the rights of national governments to exert control.'[13] The fear that Corera outlined was fuelled only further by the Snowden revelations beginning in 2013, which 'took the wind out of their [the United States] sails' and 'undermined in one stroke Washington's efforts to take the moral high ground against Chinese espionage'.[14] This in turn 'provided a boost for the Cyber Sovereignty movement'[15] by aligning non-authoritarian nations – such as Brazil and Germany – to some of the key goals in the movement like storage of data within one's own country. China should be seen as the leading voice calling for greater Cyber Sovereignty, and they have promoted its virtues at numerous diplomatic settings in recent years. Now, whenever counter-arguments to the Cyber Sovereignty model are put forward, the retort is simply that it is a deceptive ploy to further enable surveillance programmes by American intelligence services.[16]

The Chinese View: 'Technology in Service of the State'[17]

Much of the logic behind the Cyber Sovereignty concept has in turn been built on by the Cyberspace Administration of China (CAC) with their first National Cyberspace Security Strategy in 2016 that explicitly identifies the core challenges China believes it faces. The document focuses primarily on the internal challenges faced; first, political stability is viewed as under threat as cyberspace can be used

> to interfere in the internal political affairs of other countries, to attack other countries' political systems, incite social unrest, subvert other countries' regimes, as well as large-scale cyber surveillance, cyber espionage and other such activities gravely harm national political security and users' information security.[18]

Second, economic security is viewed, much like among the Western democracies, as under threat due to the relentless targeting of networks that have now become critical national infrastructures in their own right, dependent as trading financial infrastructures have become. Such attacks will instil 'paralysis' that will result in 'disastrous consequences and gravely harming national economic security and the public interest.'[19] Third are the shared concerns about cybercrime and terrorist use of cyber means, noting that activities such as data theft, intellectual property theft, and the spread of malware lead to the destruction of social security. Further, however, is a belief in the corrosion of what is termed 'cultural security', where socialist core values are undermined by the presence of online behaviours seen as obscene, violent, and superstitious. It is believed that online a 'loss of moral norms and lack of sincerity happens frequently'[20] with redress urgently needed.

What is clear already from just the internal challenges China insists it faces, particularly a belief in cultural erosion, is their broader conception of what security in cyberspace entails. Jon Lindsay sums up this conception in his excellent edited volume *China and Cybersecurity* when he states that a core distinguishing feature 'of the Chinese conception of information security (*xinxi anquan*) is that it emphasises *Internet content* as much, if not more than, technical network security (*wangluo anquan*).'[21] Barrass and Inkster are also important to note at this stage, for they point out well that for China the concept of sovereignty itself carries a more expansive meaning than in the Western understanding. They remind readers that the

Chinese word for sovereignty – *zhu quan* – is linked to the much older concept of the "mandate of heaven" – *tian ming* – and that for China sovereignty is 'not about sharing power, but about China being the uncontested sovereign in its own "world."''[22]

Cyber Sovereignty is very much concerned with the internal security of the state and establishing absolute authority within, but it does also have significant concerns about the international environment without as well. The Chinese strategy views international competition as rapidly developing, specifically noting that at the international level 'there is strife for the control of strategic resources in cyberspace, to occupy norm-setting power and strategic commanding heights, and in competition a pursuit of the strategic initiative that is growing more fierce every day.'[23] Other actors are seen as aggravating an arms race in cyberspace and bringing new challenges to global peace, without opting to name the actors in question. Consequently, French states that Chinese efforts abroad seek to impart 'the negative notion that relatively closed and authoritarian states should work together to prevent interference in their affairs by others, or even pollution by democratic values.'[24]

It is at this point that the former US State Department official Michael Pillsbury's views be consulted, for their illustration of the concerns that the Chinese themselves outline with their strategy regarding the international sphere and how they should operate. In Pillsbury's *The Hundred Year Marathon*, the title to Chapter 5 is 'America, the Great Satan' that he believes has come to form the dominant Chinese view of the American superpower. Indeed, a central argument of his book is that 'the hawks have successfully persuaded the Chinese leadership to view America as a dangerous hegemon that it must replace.'[25] Cyberspace in this view is but one battlefield in a broader campaign against American hegemony. Pillsbury further details his witnessing (during several official deployments to China since the 1960s) of Chinese perceptions of America as taught there. He states that in their version of modern history, 'the United States used trade, economic cooperation, technology transfers, diplomacy, cultural and educational exchanges, and pressure for democratic reforms to weaken the Soviet Union from within.'[26] It is activities such as these, reinforced by revelations of pervasive modern surveillance programmes, that serve to animate the Chinese concern about the international environment as stated above in their strategy. While Pillsbury must be taken with a pinch of salt as it were, direct and long-term experience of China such as his should not be discounted when it serves to contextualise views such as those established in formal Chinese strategy.

Returning to that strategy, China issued a series of principles to guide their efforts, first and foremost of which is '(1) Respecting and protecting sovereignty in cyberspace.'[27] Added to this is the top strategic task of 'Resolutely defending sovereignty in cyberspace.'[28] Tellingly this includes the explicit call to 'Resolutely oppose all actions to subvert our country's national regime or destroy our country's sovereignty through the network.'[29] All Chinese rhetoric is centrally based on the establishment and preservation of sovereignty as the core value guiding their view to the future of cyberspace development, intended primarily to secure the stability of their regime and ensure that it is sovereign nation states who are regarded as the key players in any governance regime moving ahead.

The Russian view

This view is also subscribed to by Russia, for they share a common objective that creates, as Margolin states, a 'marriage of convenience' between the two nations rather than an alliance per se: regime stability.[30] Like China, 'Russia's idea of international information security implies significant government responsibility and control over information resources.'[31] The Russian view differs from the Western in that the 'Russian government understands information sovereignty as "non-proliferation" of foreign information among Russian citizens.'[32] Indeed, so strong is Russian opposition that they do not even ascribe to the term cyber security, instead opting for "international information security" as the operating term they refer to at all times. As Moore rightly observes, one will find formal Russian strategy 'does not have the term "cyber" mentioned at all.'[33]

This term is elaborated on in the Russian-issued Convention on International Information Security, identifying as one of the main threats 'actions in the information space aimed at undermining the political, economic, and social system of another government, and psychological campaigns carried out against the population of a State with the intent of destabilizing society.'[34] Russia further strengthens its alignment with the Chinese position by declaring that state parties should enjoy 'sovereign equality,' and with it 'the right to make sovereign norms and govern its information space according to its national laws.'[35]

Like China, Russia also issued its own Information Security Doctrine[36] (rather than strategy in this case) in late 2016, albeit with slightly differing objectives. Sukhankin outlines these objectives best: 'countering external threats; overcoming the international "discrimination" of the Russian media; and eliminating the drawbacks and limitations faced by Russia in the domain of information technologies.'[37] The first objective is very much aimed at establishing total control over domestic information flows and, as Sukhankin critically identifies, the doctrine is focused less on the development of indigenous Russian technology and competitiveness, and instead 'appears to be conceived as a tool meant to control and strangulate potential sources of anti-government sentiment.'[38]

Klimburg notes that the Russian 'obsession' with foreign media and even civil society undermining their own information sphere 'shifted into high gear in the wake of the first wave of pro-democracy colour revolutions in Kyrgyzstan, Lebanon, and, most notably, Ukraine.'[39] The aforementioned fear of open access to information among the citizenry outlined in the previous chapter is the clearest dominant motivator behind China and Russia's leadership in the Cyber Sovereignty movement. Klimburg is right to insist the term "coloured revolutions" is hard to over-emphasise and that the pro-democratic movements occurring since 2010 'were profoundly frightening occurrences.'[40] China and Russia have clearly learnt the lessons from the revolutions from the early decade and Internet freedom,[41] with Cyber Sovereignty the overarching strategy in preventing this history from repeating itself in either Russia or the Chinese mainland.

For both China and Russia, the belief is that 'national security – read regime security – is not attainable until "informational security" is established.'[42] In order to gain the diplomatic traction required for Cyber Sovereignty to become accepted, China and Russia also both seek to draw other nations into the belief set. Inkster perhaps puts this best with regards to the Chinese in arguing that 'The country has in effect embarked on a global experiment in which liberal democracies serve as the control group.'[43] For this, 'China seeks to establish a narrative wherein state power already exists in the cyber realm, but where the USA is a hegemon.'[44] Herein lies a core weakness not only of the Cyber Sovereignty concept as a whole, but also of the stability of the "marriage of convenience" enjoyed with Russia and any other subscriber to Cyber Sovereignty; the closeness of these relationships is 'not dependent on their ties with each other, but is defined in relation to the US.'[45] This critical aspect must be recognised as a diplomatic opportunity for the Western liberal model if there is to be a sustained attempt to counter, for theirs is no true "alliance" but only a convergence of general interest motivated by fear.

The view from international law

Despite the aforementioned diplomatic weakness to the Cyber Sovereignty model, a level of credence is provided to its case from building opinion in international legal circles. Currently, emerging opinion is that current international law does indeed apply to activities in cyberspace, crucially with little need to amend existing provisions. This point was highlighted in the American 2011 International Strategy for Cyberspace itself:

> The development of norms for state conduct in cyberspace does not require a reinvention of customary international law, nor does it render

existing international norms obsolete. Long-standing international norms guiding State behaviour – in times of peace and conflict – also apply in cyberspace.[46]

This is a view that is also shared through the much-vaunted *Tallinn Manuals* from NATO's Cooperative Cyber Defence Centre of Excellence (CCDCOE). The first manual considered a wide range of opinion on the applicability of laws in conflict; the second – following the same model of wide-ranging consultation with two International Groups of Experts – is devoted to the applicability of laws during peacetime activities. Both manuals seek to impart a series of rules to help guide thinking and behaviour. Rule 1 is the belief that 'A State may exercise control over cyber infrastructure and activities within its sovereign territory.'[47] This rule is reinforced in the second manual that simply says, 'The principle of State sovereignty applies in cyberspace.'[48]

Both manuals elaborate on this principle: 'In particular, States enjoy sovereignty over any cyber infrastructure located on their territory and activities associated with that cyber infrastructure.'[49] That sovereign status comes with two consequences, first 'that cyber infrastructure is subject to both legal and regulatory control by the State. Second, the State's territorial sovereignty protects such cyber infrastructure.'[50] That infrastructure is clearly established, 'the physical, logical, and social layers or cyberspace are encompassed in the principle of sovereignty.'[51] Further to this, with *2.0*'s second rule, a strong hand is lent to the Cyber Sovereignty cause: 'A state enjoys sovereign authority with regard to the cyber infrastructure, persons, and cyber activities located within its territory, *subject to its international legal obligations.*'[52]

This second rule establishes a belief in the exercise of internal sovereignty by the state. With it, 'a State is free to adopt any measure it considers necessary or appropriate with regard to cyber infrastructure, persons engaged in cyber activities, or cyber activities themselves within its territory.'[53] Importantly for the section to follow on data localisation legislation being enacted in various forms globally, 'the State may promulgate and enforce domestic laws and regulations regarding them.'[54] With such powers, the state may 'restrict, in part or in whole, access to cyberspace within its territory, *in particular to certain online content.*'[55] This is no doubt a crucial element for states like China and Russia, who define their national security by the information sphere as much as, if not more than, they do territorial integrity itself.

As a consequence of these realities, however, it is also recognised that there are limitations on sovereign authority, reflecting the truth that sovereignty is never absolute. Customary or treaty law is held as a restricting element in the exercise of sovereign rights. 'For example . . . a State's sovereignty in the territorial sea, archipelagic waters or straits used for international navigation is limited under customary international law by the rights of innocent passage, archipelagic sea lanes passage, and transit passage, respectively.'[56] In essence, what the manual is saying is that while a state can exercise authority over its particular *jurisdiction* of cyberspace, it cannot do so over cyberspace itself *per se*, exactly in the same manner that a state can exercise sovereign authority over territorial waters but not lay claim to the ocean itself.

The manuals establish two caveats to their contents very well; first are those seen above about restrictions according to established customary law that guards against absolute sovereignty being exercised. Second is the self-acknowledgment from the manuals themselves that is worth quoting at length:

> The manual does not represent the views of the NATO CCD COE, its sponsoring nations, or NATO. In particular, it is not meant to reflect NATO doctrine. Nor does it reflect the position of any organisation or State represented by observers.[57]

Despite these well-established acknowledgments, one must assess that the *Tallinn Manual* projects provide a strong foundation on which the Cyber Sovereignty movement can rest its case, for three core reasons:

1   International legal opinion believes strongly in the principle of state sovereignty over its jurisdiction's cyberspace.
2   That opinion further believes in the state's authority to make and enforce domestic law pertinent to the proper regulation of infrastructure, persons, and content, however subjective may be the state's view of appropriateness.
3   Logically, sovereignty must be established over cyberspace in some form, for the traditional components of international law to remain and to prevent the risk of an anarchic space developing.

Data localisation laws

Armed now with the necessary understanding of international legal opinion on the place of sovereignty in cyberspace, focus can turn to a clear manifestation of how Cyber Sovereignty is developing, which is via data localisation legislation. Data localisation, very simply, 'can be defined as the act of storing data on a device that is physically located within the country where the data was created.'[58] There are many reasons cited for why this is required, with cyber security offered as the paramount reason, 'which are intended to keep citizen's personal data in-country and subject to local regulation.'[59] In this author's opinion, however, the enactment of data localisation is the most prescient measure being taken to assert state sovereignty over cyberspace, as well as an indicator of the broadening appeal of at least core elements of the Cyber Sovereignty movement to other nations. That is, that the imperative behind such laws is certainly politically motivated rather than concerned with the optimisation of technical efficiency online.

Before citing the examples of such laws from Russia and China, it is hugely important to note that many other nations are also bringing similar – if less demanding – legislation into practice. Vietnam approved their *Cybersecurity Law* in June 2018, due to take effect from 2019, despite representation from big tech firms like Facebook and Google, as well as rights groups and even concerns from the United States government. That law requires companies to both set up offices and store data within Vietnam itself, increasing the demand on Facebook and Google in particular, as they did not already have an office-based presence in the country.[60]

India, the world's largest democracy, has also taken similar measures with the *Personal Data Protection Bill, 2018*. So far, Indian efforts have remained focused on implementation with regards to financial transaction information, with the Reserve Bank of India issuing a notification that requires all "payment system providers" to store all payments data exclusively in India.[61] Yet this is not expected to be the limit of the legislation, with the RBI's notice representing merely the first move of a 'ban on the international transfer of data generated by Indian ecommerce users.'[62]

Likewise, in the UK, the *Investigatory Powers Act, 2016* has proven contentious, being commonly dubbed the "snoopers charter" due to the support it provides to law enforcement and intelligence services. The most important points of the bill to note are:

- The requirement for Internet service providers (as well as other communications service providers operating in the UK) to retain all user information for a period of 12 months in order to facilitate law enforcement access if necessary.[63]
- British intelligence services will be permitted to continue the practice of so-called "bulk data sets" so long as this is done in a legal and proportionate manner.[64]
- It permits the practice of equipment interference by law enforcement and the intelligence services throughout the course of their duties.[65]

Russia has a far more expansive legislation in place, Federal Law No. 242-FZ[66] that went into effect on 1 September 2015. This personal data law requires 'all domestic and foreign companies to accumulate, store, and process personal information on Russian citizens on servers physically located within Russian borders.'[67] This is a crucial element in making the Russian application far more expansive, for it takes their practice beyond the normal conception of data localisation being about data created *within* a nation to asserting authority over all Russian citizens' information no matter where that information has been generated. This 'applies with equal force to companies based outside of Russia,'[68] with penalties for violation including the blocking of one's website and services.

This is particularly important because a major global firm has already incurred such a ban, LinkedIn. In late 2016, reports emerged from Russian users of the service that access was no longer permitted, with Russian regulators banning the platform.[69] That regulator, *Roskomnadzor*, simply stated that in their view 'The company refused to comply with the requirement to localise databases with personal data of Russian citizens on the territory of the Russian Federation, thus confirming their disinterest in working on the Russian market.'[70]

Further actions to reinforce control in Russia have included a ban on virtual private networks (VPNs), which are very popular measures for an individual to encrypt their own devices' communications and mask their IP address. This ban went into effect in November 2017 with Leonid Levin, then head of the Russian State Duma's information policy committee, quoted as saying the law is not intended to ban all users, but simply access to "unlawful content".[71]

China has also implemented similar measures to those in Russia, with its own Cybersecurity Law that came into effect in June 2017. This law requires 'network operators to cooperate with Chinese crime or security investigations and allow full access to data and unspecified "technical support" to the authorities on request.'[72] Article 37 of the law establishes the need to store data in mainland China, which also adopts the Russian view on data relating to Chinese citizens. Data that is gathered or produced by network operators in China must be stored in China, likewise business or other data gathered on Chinese citizens is to be kept 'on domestic servers and not transferred abroad without permission.'[73] Deliberately broad in scope, *Forbes* describes interpreting the law in its full detail as 'mind boggling', noting further that they believe it is impossible for companies to be compliant via their own interpretation and that understanding will need to come from regulators and how they practice the law domestically in China. 'Moreover, the presence of multiple industry regulators will result in patchy interpretation, conflicting signals and unpredictable enforcement.'[74] *The Financial Times* rightly noted that 'Multinationals will be hardest hit, as the data localisation measures prevent them pooling client data in cloud storage databases across the world.'[75]

For a clear example of a major corporation needing to make dramatic changes to their data storage model, one need look no further than Apple. In a move to ensure compliance with local laws, since 2017 Apple has shifted the storage of its iCloud data on Chinese users to a China-based company, Guizhou-Cloud Big Data, for storage in mainland China.[76] While Apple has been insistent that user data still has significant privacy safeguard in place, critics have responded with the point that Apple is also required to store the necessary cryptographic keys in China as well.[77] This has proven highly controversial, leading to charges of hypocrisy against Apple by Amnesty International, who accuse the tech giant of putting profits above their own self-declared belief in privacy as a human right.[78] Actions such as Apple's capitulation (or adherence depending on one's viewpoint) to Chinese law of course are made while Tim Cook – the "privacy martyr" – continues to issue warnings such as those at his address to a conference of European privacy commissioners in Brussels in October 2018. There he warned about the 'data industrial complex' and 'Platforms and algorithms that praise to improve our lives can actually magnify our worst human tendencies.' Importantly, Cook states that 'Now, more than ever . . . we must ask ourselves a fundamental question: What kind of world do we want to live in?'[79] Apple's rhetoric is no doubt laudable, but actions such as the decision to abide with data localisation in China betray a strong inconsistency between rhetoric on privacy and deeds practiced equally worldwide, as well as highlighting the power dynamics between one of the big tech firms and state authority moving ahead.

Additionally, to the data localisation provisions in Chinese law, China has also mirrored Russian actions in imposing a ban on VPNs as well. In 2017, the Chinese government issued notice to the three primary telecoms providers – China Mobile, China Unicom, and China Telecom – to bar the use of VPNs by 1 February 2018.[80] Ostensibly, this has been done primarily to prevent their use in bypassing censorship controls but is seen as a major escalation of already extensive censorship in the country.[81] This has been part of a 14-month "cleanup" of Internet access services in China, all designed to create 'an interlocking framework of laws, regulations, and standards'[82] that make it even harder to circumvent the much lauded "Great Firewall" of China.[83]

Ultimately, data localisation is a clear example, though by no means exclusively so, of sovereignty asserting itself on to cyberspace. By instilling political demand for data to be localised, rather than globally dispersed as is more technically optimal,[84] states are presenting data-driven businesses with a clear choice, 'a big choice for big tech' to adopt Mayer-Schonberger and Ramge's phrase:[85] abide by local law or be denied access to our market. Accepting the latter no doubt imperils the successful growth of any business into international markets and is a key point of leverage now being wielded by states. As a result, businesses now face a tricky position, much like that Apple has already been criticised for: trying to stand up for human rights (especially the belief that free Internet access and privacy is a part of that) while also accepting the rule of law where one does business. Consequently, state sovereignty is already imposing itself through laws such as those detailed above through varying degrees, with Russia and China proving the most stringent. Despite this, however, it must be remembered that the democracies too are imposing sovereign authority, with the UK's controversial Investigatory Powers Act conveying significant powers to the state's ability to ensure security. These practices lend strong credence all around to the notion that, in varying forms the world over, sovereignty will find its way into cyberspace.

2.3 The Free Internet Coalition

One would be under the impression that the ideas that spawned both cyberspace and the Internet itself would form a coherent argument to be aired; unfortunately, readers will find that this is not the case. That this is not so is also a contributory reason for the insecurities encountered in cyberspace and the uncertainties over its future. What one will encounter instead is a milieu of clunky and ultimately ineffective terminology, such as "multistakeholderism," "Internet Freedom," the "rules of the road," the "free flow of information," and an updated view of the "liberating promise of technology," among others. The strange truth is that there has never been a coherent, politically driven view from the liberal West as to what the future of cyberspace would be; it was simply accepted as a self-evident reality that the peaceful rise of the Internet would be unstoppable and that liberal values would inherently remain at its heart. When one accepts this state of illpreparedness on the part of previous generations, one is able to empathise closer with the challenges faced by the liberal nations today, what Klimburg terms the Free Internet Coalition,[86] in trying to counter the rise of the Cyber Sovereignty movement.

The apolitical origins of the liberal view

> Governments of the industrial world, you weary giants of flesh and steel, I come from cyberspace, the new home of Mind. On behalf of the future, I ask you of the past to leave us alone. You are not welcome among us. You have no sovereignty where we gather.
>   We have no elected government, nor are we likely to have one, so I address you with no greater authority than that with which liberty itself

always speaks. I declare the global social space we are building to be naturally independent of the tyrannies you seek to impose on us. You have no
moral right to rule us nor do you possess any true methods of enforcement
we have true reason to fear.[87]

The need to indulge such a long quotation from Barlow's 1996 *Declaration
on the Independence of Cyberspace* is to remind everyone of the types of
views that were strongly prevalent in the early heyday of the Internet, views
that seem not only impossible today but also catastrophically wrong. Barlow declared cyberspace as being beyond not only the authority of states,
but also beyond their enforcement mechanisms. It was an affirmation of a
future view where the individual is above all the most empowered person;
the connected individual, with unrestricted global access to information,
falling back on newfound tools like public-key encryption (PGP) to ensure
their privacy. At the heart of such thinking was an almost pure form of libertarianism that had finally found its most potent mix of tools – 'computers,
networks, and public keys'[88] – for furthering the liberty of any individuals
who could command computer literacy.

Before elaborating on what and how the Free Internet Coalition hopes to
achieve, it is necessary to very briefly examine exactly why the Internet was
left to a state of relative *laissez faire* through the early post-Cold War period
that gave rise to views such as Barlow's. This relates back to the core reasons why in America the Internet was supported to grow as it was, and here
it is best to revisit the role of the then Senator Al Gore. Al Gore has become
a near punch line in the history of the Internet, as Runciman captures well:
'People laugh when Al Gore claims to have invented the Internet. So they
should.'[89] Such levity, however, detracts from his actual role in helping to
create what he termed the "information superhighway." A line of initiatives
instigated and supported by Gore from 1986 led to the opening up of the
Internet to the masses, culminating in the explosion of access that came in
the summer of 1993. It began with a congressional study in 1986 on how
to open up the research networks that were the mainstay of the Internet
at the time, which progressed to the High Performance Computing Act of
1991 and the Scientific and Advanced Technology Act of 1992. These acts
allowed companies like AOL to connect to the research networks for the
first time; this was swiftly followed by the Information Infrastructure Act of
1993 that enabled public access and the commercialisation of cyberspace.[90]

The point of this very brief digression into the initial pathway of opening
the Internet to the masses is to reveal a plainly evident and simple truth, to
governments the Internet was opened as an *economic enabler*, a superhighway that would spur above all greater commercial opportunity and growth.

These actions were taken at a time where small government was seen as king, with regulation needed only as far as to open opportunity for the capitalist economic model to go to work online. There was little serious anticipation or expectation of the scale of cybercrime and insecurity that would result. And there was most certainly not a coherent political view of how cyberspace should be governed beyond its existing technical governance mechanisms; as a result, 'a mythical, libertarian origin story arose, which fed the belief that the Internet is so open that regulation is unnecessary.'[91] Indeed, the liberal view was one that was built entirely on this assumption that that helps clarify the difficulties and even confusion that one encounters when trying to decipher what the liberal view of a so-called free Internet actually is.

What the Free Internet Coalition hopes to achieve

There are three primary arenas that can be deduced from the liberal view of cyberspace's future, each of which is an expression of a core liberal value: the Open Internet (expressive of inclusivity), Internet Freedom (expressive of liberty), and the Rule of Law (expressive of justice) as the core components. First is the concept of the Open Internet, which also encompasses a more commonly known position in practice, Net Neutrality. Open Internet effectively comprises two features, technical and political. From the technical standpoint is the view that 'every device on the Internet should be able to exchange data packets with any other device that was willing to receive them.'[92] Universal connectivity underwritten by open technical standards is the essence of the view in this regard. Additionally, when it comes to Net Neutrality, the political belief is that all data should be treated as equal, in order to ensure maximum participation online without disenfranchising those with additional financial costs; it is the view that 'any content . . . can't be constrained.'[93]

Despite being challenged domestically within the US in recent years, the Open Internet has been given fresh reaffirmation by the Federal Communications Commission (FCC) with their Restoring Internet Freedom Order[94] that became active on 11 June 2018. The liberal value inherent in the Open Internet is the concept of inclusivity, to ensure an equality of opportunity among all individuals, none of whom is to be prejudiced in their pursuits through a lack of access. With the United Nations also affirming Internet access as a human right in 2016,[95] it is a clear pursuit of the Free Internet Coalition to ensure that the Open Internet in both a technical and political sense continues. All machines should be able to use open technical standards, and all data should remain treated equally.

Second, the Free Internet Coalition seeks to ensure the continued pursuit of Internet Freedom, which relates to the expression of liberty through the acceptance of basic human rights online. The rights of access, freedom of expression, and privacy and the provision of technologies to circumvent censors lie at the heart of Internet Freedom and are a clear expression of the concept of liberty through cyberspace. At present, American efforts to support Internet Freedom are politically neutral, supporting an expansion of the "Freedom to Connect" ideal globally rather than explicitly supporting connectivity and rights across authoritarian nations.[96]

Finally, the Rule of Law is key to ensuring that justice as a component of liberalism is assured. This has been laid out well by various initiatives, including various pieces of domestic legislation that have already been mentioned earlier, but in terms of international consensus it was well labelled by the then British Foreign Secretary William Hague. Hague labelled the pursuit as finding the "rules of the road" to develop agreed norms of behaviour in cyberspace, highlighting the need to target not only clear threats such as cyber attacks but also 'the threat against individual rights to freedom of expression' and the recognition that the 'free flow of information is an essential underpinning of liberty.'[97] Britain also captured this sentiment well in the 2011 Cyber Security Strategy, where in the dominating vision for the achievement of cyber security it declared that all actions would be guided by the values of 'liberty, fairness, transparency and the rule of law.'[98]

While a messy affair without central coherence, leadership, or at times even comprehensive articulation from the liberal democracies, one can effectively capture the essential requisites of the Free Internet Coalition through the pursuit of inclusivity, liberty, and justice. The protection of these three core arenas through Open Internet, Internet Freedom, and the Rule of Law are crucial components in ensuring the continued centrality of liberal values in and through cyberspace.

The failure of the UN GGE

The place of consideration for the primary diplomatic effort at seeking international consensus for behaviour online lies at the United Nations. The UN has convened several Group of Government Experts sessions since 2004 on the issue of cyber security, yet it notably collapsed in 2017, leaving an uncertain future for diplomatic talks in this space. Previous work had established the application of the principles of international law and the UN Charter in cyberspace, as well the agreement that the pursuit of non-binding norms for responsible state behaviour could reduce risks to international peace.[99]

While there have been numerous other diplomatic efforts over the years, it is the collapse of the GGE in 2017 that has raised serious questions about where diplomatic progress on the future of cyber security will now come from. The leader of the US delegation to the GGE, Michele Markoff, released a statement in the aftermath of the collapse berating 'those who are unwilling to affirm the applicability of these international legal rules and principles,' with such countries believing that they 'are free to act in or through cyberspace . . . with no limits or constraints on their actions. . . . This is a dangerous and unsupportable view.'[100]

Two core narratives have emerged to explain the breakdown of the GGE, the first focuses on the intransigence of Cuba late in the process, who argued that proceeding as outlined would lead to a militarisation of cyberspace because of the right to self-defence included in the UN Charter, insisting instead on seeking peaceful resolution to disputes.[101] The other narrative is that the difference of positions between those for Cyber Sovereignty and those for the Free Internet Coalition are simply irreconcilable, creating a natural impasse that neither side can yet move in their favour.[102]

Korzak correctly highlights two key diplomatic consequences that are highly concerning for the Free Internet Coalition moving ahead. First, 'it leaves us with an unresolved international legal debate where the viewpoints seem to be diverging and solidifying rather than converging.' Second is simply the question of how diplomacy will now continue.[103] This is a very concerning position, because while diplomacy to shape acceptable international standards and norms stagnates, the continued occurrence of cyber security events in the vein of WannaCry and Not-Petya all help the Cyber Sovereignty advocates in 'making headway with their core wish: the framing of information as a weapon.'[104] Further to this is also Kissinger's warning that the road to any acceptable world order can enjoy no meaningful progress 'if one of the most pervasive elements of international life is excluded from serious dialogue.'[105]

Where does the Free Internet Coalition go from here?

With the failure to date of diplomatic efforts at building a consensus on acceptable behaviour across cyberspace by state actors, and the growth in the ability of authoritarian states to utilise cyber tools with greater effect as outlined above, the question must be raised as to how the Free Internet Coalition now progresses. Answering this question necessitates longer term principles for action, rather than any intricate and immediate diplomatic plan. Ultimately, however, it requires a major reassertion of leadership, particularly from the United States, if any vestige of a liberal cyberspace is to endure into the future.

i. Revisit the social contract

> [I]t will be equally forgotten that the vigor of government is essential to the security of liberty; that, in the contemplation of a sound and well-informed judgment, their interest can never be separated.[106]

While it may seem strange to revisit such a fundamental component of lib-eralism, it is argued here that the challenges to the liberal vision of the future for cyberspace run far deeper than the technological insecurities pre-sented by contemporary events. Instead, the scale of disruption encountered between the relationship of the individual and the state, before mentioning relations between states, necessitates a re-examination of the basic social contract that exists between the individual and their respective state. In the classical sense of the social contract in the Rousseau tradition, it is the crea-tion of a 'moral collective body'[107] from the masses that is key to legiti-mising the agreement between how far powers are exercised over liberty in the pursuit of security. In essence, the basic understanding from liberal theory has been that one commands liberty in as far as one's exercising of liberty does not harm that of another. Furthermore, in order to help establish rights and the security of the moral collective body, the people engage in an implicit contract with the state, whereby a level of rights are sacrificed (or permitted to be intruded upon) in order to ensure the provision of security.

Wittes and Blum are very effective in outlining that the traditional way of viewing this relationship between liberty and security is flawed, because it implies they are ultimately separate entities from each other. The idea of balance has traditionally been offered to highlight a tension between two objectives of government, ensuring liberty and security together.[108] Yet the idea of balance risks miscategorising the relationship between security and liberty as one of opposites requiring careful balance, when in fact the rela-tionship is symbiotic. The opening quote to this section, from Alexander Hamilton's Federalist Paper No. 1, is key in emphasising that the symbiosis between liberty and security is ultimately inseparable in their interests and that a strong hand from government is needed – particularly during times of significant disruption – to ensure that the interests of both are served. Bal-ance is a flawed concept even before trying to apply it to the technological disruption wrought by cyberspace;[109] instead, an acceptance of symbiosis is necessary.

This flaw has been manifested in clear fashion in Britain during the dis-putes between groups such as Privacy International and the British govern-ment over the adoption of the Investigatory Powers Act. A strong debate about the intrusive powers allocated to law enforcement and intelligence services is ultimately misguided, for it fails to recognise the inherent neces-sity of ensuring the security of the collective in order to preserve liberty. Instead, such debate should shift away from concerns over tactical affairs such as exactly what powers are legally permitted in which country, and instead begin to shift focus to a broader discussion in liberal democratic societies about what now is the relationship between liberty and security in a world with cyberspace?

In any society, citizens rightly expect certain allocations from its government, the preservation of its liberties but also fundamentally their security from external attack and wanton criminality from within. For European states, social welfare is also afforded so that citizens are afforded protection from the worst of conditions befalling them. This was best put by one of the fathers of the British welfare state, William Beveridge, with his simple statement, 'A starving man is not free.'[110] Total freedom would also include the freedom to starve, which would logically be illiberal. The point of this exploration therefore is to highlight a guiding truth that should be evident and central to any liberal conception of cyberspace, *the freedom to be attacked or subjugated in cyberspace is no freedom at all*. Much like the addition of cyberspace into Article 19 of the UN Declaration on Human Rights, in liberal societies there should be a reaffirmation of what rights and protections citizens can expect from their government as part of the social contract in cyberspace. Benkler was quite right to note in 2006 that we are now in the midst of a transformation across technological, economic, and organisational affairs that provides the opportunity to 'renegotiate the terms of freedom, justice, and productivity in the information society.'[111] In a space where it is very difficult to find consensus over appropriate behaviour, to curtail problems like cybercrime but also incessant cyber bullying and "trolling," it is necessary for citizens to be reminded of the social contract, with their rights spelled out in far plainer terms than is done via legislation. As Benkler argues, missing such an opportunity to enrich democracy, freedom, and justice 'would be unforgivable.'[112]

ii. Accept there are other political positions on cyberspace

A core contention of this work has been the resurgence of political views into cyberspace, mirroring the rise of multipolar challenges to the immediate post-Cold War victory that the liberal democracies enjoyed. Indeed, it has sought to be shown throughout that a large part of the reason behind the lack of coherent liberal vision for the future of cyberspace has been the historical lack of challenge to their view; there simply was no clear challenger to necessitate creating a rigorous position behind which to mobilise popular opinion; it was taken as a self-evident reality.

Such self-evident reality is certainly no more, the apolitical honeymoon is over, and for a liberal vision of the Internet to survive it is also necessary to begin accepting the actual realities of the geopolitical order. That reality is very simply that there are significant challenges and challengers to the liberal world order, who have their own vision in Cyber Sovereignty for how the future of cyberspace and the Internet should proceed. A sensible policy to pursue the liberal vision must also accept the reality that other political orders do exist, indeed they thrive and pose a genuine threat to the values held dear and taken for granted among the Western nations.

In this vein, it is important to heed the views of Mearshimer, with his insistence that 'Liberal states have a crusader mentality hard wired into them that is hard to restrain.'[113] The temptation to forcibly export liberal values has been seen many times in strategic history, most recently in the period of the 9/11 wars in the unsuccessful attempt to socially reengineer nations away from dictatorship and tribal feudalism in Iraq and Afghanistan, respectively. Mearshimer is not being a pure pessimist in arguing that liberal hegemony is an ambitious strategy that is also destined to fail.[114] The ambitions after 9/11 overstretched even the American hyper power of the moment, revealing the truth that no power is absolute in the global system. This reality needs also to be heeded in the battles for the future of cyberspace.

Ultimately, the argument of Mearshimer should be a clear focal point in conditioning liberal views to a realistic proposition, when he argues that powerful states can only pursue hegemony in a unipolar moment. 'When the world is bipolar or multipolar, on the other hand, great powers have little choice but to act according to realist dictates, because of the presence of rival powers.'[115] The world is no longer unipolar, the broader multipolar geopolitical reality will also affect cyberspace, which represents one front in the broader geopolitical competition of the twenty-first century. A sensible strategy for pursuing the liberal vision must accept and account for the very real challenge it now faces, and own up to its false assumption that the Internet was an inherently liberal technology; achieving such an accommodation of political diversity 'will take a surge of strategic imagination'[116] that has been lacking and is sorely needed, for it has been certainly proven that other political orders have found applications to the technology that was assumed would organically liberate their masses from within.

iii. Focus on allies and structures

This program must light the path to peace and order among nations in a system based on freedom and justice, as envisaged in the Charter of the United Nations. Further, it must envisage the political and economic measures with which and the military shield behind which the free world can work to frustrate the Kremlin design by the strategy of the cold war . . . The only sure victory lies in the frustration of the Kremlin design by the steady development of the moral and material strength of the free world and its projection into the Soviet world in such a way as to bring about an internal change in the Soviet system.[117]

While this author is deeply wary of the place of analogies, especially Cold War-centric ones, when applied to cyberspace, the place of NSC-68 is highly pertinent for inspiration to creating a strategic path for the liberal vision for the future of the Internet. NSC-68 was instrumental in establishing the thought base for a grand strategy against the Soviet Union, with the extended quote above showing how its strategic acumen has certainly stood the test of time, and indeed also correctly identified the broader elements beyond military forces that were needed for the mobilisation of allies, which is sorely needed today.

It can be argued that the Cold War structures established by the United States for the Cold War – such as the United Nations and the International Monetary Fund – are soft implements in a liberal order that is actually a myth, as had been argued by Graham Allison, who refers to the notion of such institutions underpinning peace during the Cold War as 'conceptual Jell-o.'[118] Yet despite such a critical view, it is necessary in the twenty-first century to recognise the importance of such structures in mobilising, as NSC-68 called for, the nations of the free world in collective opposition to alternative views that seek to undermine and fracture liberal values.

For the Free Internet Coalition to prosper and mount a serious counter against the Cyber Sovereignty movement, an effort akin to that of NSC-68 is required that recognises the need for a programme to unify liberal democracies based on the collective and shared values that they hold of equality, liberty, and justice. Indeed, if Allison is to be believed that the liberal order is a myth, one must question why those institutional elements comprising the order are the targets of such systematic undermining by non-liberal nations in current times. It is certainly a recognition on their part that the 'sure victory' envisaged by NSC-68 came about through the 'frustrations' of Kremlin designs that collective moral strength expressed through international institutions enabled and needs to be prevented from happening again in order for Cyber Sovereignty to prevail.

Recognising this would allow a focus on allies and building a programme for a future vision of cyberspace utilising existing and perhaps even creating new institutions – such as Fried and Polyakova's "Counter-Disinformation Coalition"[119] – that would aim at the persistent frustration of the Cyber Sovereignty proponents who oppose the Free Internet Coalition. By securing and mobilising the collective moral strength of liberal democracies once more, the Free Internet Coalition could embrace a different position to that of Allison, that 'The order is far from a myth; it is the United States' most important competitive advantage.'[120] Such a view would in fact be far closer to an accepting and building upon the belief of General James T. Mattis, when he labelled the post-war creation of institutions and rules-based international order 'the greatest gift of the greatest generation.'[121]

iv. Declare red lines

> Interference, by armed force, with ships of Israeli flags exercising free and
> innocent passage of the Gulf of Aqaba and through the Straits of Tiran will
> be regarded by Israel as an attack entitling it to exercise its inherent right of
> self-defence under Article 51 of the Charter.[122]

This leading quote declaring Israel's position regarding any activity to
impede shipping via the Gulf of Aqaba, following the withdrawal of the
UN Emergency Force following the 1956 Suez Crisis, is the perfect place to
consider the declaration of political red lines. The drawing of red lines can
be a dicey arena indeed for political leaders, as one is banking one's credibility should they not be enforced. This is most clearly seen by President
Obama's declared red line over the Syrian civil war that severe consequences
would follow any use of chemical weapons, which were subsequently not
enforced, greatly undermining US credibility internationally.[123]

Yet what is instructive of the Israeli example is something that should
be remembered in the cyber age: the declaration of red lines is most assur-
edly a political decision. It is a decision about what is politically tolerable
to a state, and ideally represents a fair, proportionate, yet robust response
that signals a deterrent to those who might seek to cross such a line. In
cyberspace, these red lines have so far been absent, yet the events that have
included election interference since 2016 have gone far in putting the Western nations on the path to declaring such red lines. This can be most clearly
seen by the British Prime Minister Theresa May. In November 2017, Prime
Minister May delivered a speech targeting Russia, warning that 'the international order as we know it . . . is in danger of being eroded.' Specifically,
May used her speech to send the Russian state a clear message:

> We know what you are doing. And you will not succeed. Because you
> underestimate the resilience of our democracies . . . and the commit-
> ment of Western nations to the alliances that bind us. The UK will do
> what is necessary to protect ourselves, and work with our allies to do
> likewise.[124]

While not declaring a red line in the spirit of Israel involving the use of
force and invoking the right to self-defence, it is clear that the age of non-
attribution in cyberspace is ending among nation states.

In order to continue a logical path for the security of the Free Internet
Coalition, red lines will have to be developed that are credible in asserting
what is not tolerable. As things currently stand, Prime Minister May's statement implies that the British red line is the use of cyber means to subvert the

democratic process itself; such a position must be made far more explicit, combined with credible actions that can be taken to enact punitive measures when red lines are indeed crossed. Sensible establishment of red lines would consider the following: subversion of democratic processes, interference in elections, the exploitation of open and free media and press, the theft of intellectual property, the support or acquiescence of cyber criminals, and targeting of state military services and critical national infrastructure. While seemingly sensible and obvious, it is clear from the failure of diplomatic efforts like the UN GGE to establish even acceptance of existing international law that such lines do not currently exist. In the absence of clear multi-lateral diplomatic acceptance, it is up to the members of the Free Internet Coalition to begin building diplomatic norms through the establishment of their own red lines in the meantime.

v. Challenge bad behaviour

> Bad men need nothing more to compass their ends, than that good men should look on and do nothing.[125]

No strategy can be complete without action, for after all strategy is not an intellectual but a 'how to do it study, a guide to accomplishing something and doing it efficiently.'[126] The vision of the Free Internet Coalition at this stage involves not war-like behaviour, but instead a progressive strategy akin to the mobilisation of moral strength that NSC-68 called for during the Cold War. Achieving this requires not only mobilisation behind a collectively understood vision of the application of liberal values in cyberspace, but also the utilisation of alliances and structures like those that served during the Cold War to challenge contrary behaviour. Without such challenges, any pretence of defending a rules-based international order will remain a vanity rather than a seriously cherished policy position.

The challenging of bad behaviour should build on far more than simply the prospective red lines outlined above, they should also look to further liberal values by continuing to target behaviours including censorship, the blocking of journalists, Internet penetration restrictions, the protection of Internet access as a human right, the distribution of fake news, even aspects of social justice such as the education of girls in STEM subjects pertinent to cyberspace, for one example. While continuing to challenge clear violations such as subversion of democratic processes and intellectual property theft from Western corporations, the mobilisation of collective liberal moral strength must also involve the challenging of behaviours through and via cyberspace seen as contrary to liberal values. Such challenges should be made not only against nation states, but also against private corporations as well over such areas as cyber bullying, the rightful use of personal data, and the treatment of users as commercial commodities that places profits over morals.

In conclusion, the Free Internet Coalition – a far more effective term than multi-stakeholderism – has suffered a key problem in its development, *victory bred complacency*. The victory of the liberal democratic order led to a rise of triumphalism, one aspect of which was that the rise of the Internet was seen as not only an inherently liberal technology but also one that would irresistibly spread liberal values worldwide. As a consequence, there was little attempt to ever clarify what the liberal political vision was for how cyberspace should continue to develop and be governed, because it was seen as a self-evident truth that liberalism would prevail, and such articulation was simply not needed.

This section has sought to draw out the key elements of a messy and unarticulated premise from the Free Internet Coalition and offer a political coherent approach for how to counter the challenge that has emerged from the Cyber Sovereignty movement. In this an agreement emerges with Deneen's view that was is needed is 'Not a better theory, but better practices'[127] in more tangibly articulating, asserting, and building a support base behind the liberal values that the Internet once self-evidently expressed, but which now require defending and promoting in the face of Cyber Sovereignty. Without such articulation, combined with the defence and promotion of these core values, not only do the liberal democracies risk losing the battle for the future of cyberspace, but they also risk the compromise of their societies at home. Mounk expresses this risk well in noting that with the rise of populist movements, we are seeing 'the rise of *illiberal democracy*, or democracy without rights, and *undemocratic liberalism*, or rights without democracy.'[128] This broader political trend would no doubt only be exacerbated further without proactivity on the core front of the information flows in cyberspace.

This leads to one last core consideration, which is the place of trust. With the rampant rise of fake news, combined with Russian active measures to undermine truth itself, trust is increasingly compromised across most facets of life. Botsman is ultimately correct in her assertion that improving the level of trust in society not only requires greater technical safeguards and policies, it also requires individuals to act once more in the use of critical faculties. 'To ask the right questions and to seek the right information that helps us decide: is this person, information, or thing worthy of my trust?'[129] Establishing trust once more requires a wholesale campaign against the post-truth world and bizarre concepts like "alternative facts," for trust must be built on a foundation of factual understanding. Snyder expresses this well by reminding all that the relationship between equality and truth is tender and fragile. 'Communications among citizens depends upon equality. At the same time, *equality cannot be achieved without facts.*'[130] For the Free Internet Coalition to prosper, trust needs to be rebuilt within and among the citizenry of democratic nations, and also between democratic nations in order to underwrite the shared values with which to challenge Cyber Sovereignty.

Ultimately, the Free Internet Coalition requires a major reassertion of political leadership, most especially from the United States. Kornbluh is right to note the absence of US leadership online, and that it is high time for 'Washington to overcome its techno-utopian belief that the Internet can fix itself'[131] and instead begin to engage in active steps as outlined above. 'It is time, then, for the United States to reassert leadership on the global stage,'[132] but in a fashion even wider than that asserted by Flournoy and Sulmeyer, whose call is to focus more on protective measures. With the very vision for the Internet as it was originally conceived under concerted campaigns both of broad political challenge and attack through the undermining of truth itself, the need is for far-ranging political leadership that seeks to rebuild trust and faith in the liberal vision for cyberspace once more. To take it from a once assumed self-evident reality to a recognition that there 'is nothing inevitable about democracy'[133] and that, like the protection of liberal values elsewhere in daily life, so too it needs to be protected in and throughout cyberspace. Above all, it needs to be recognised that without the leadership of the United States at the forefront, any such attempt is highly likely to fail.

Notes

1 Michael N. Schmitt (ed.), *Tallinn Manual 2.0 on the International Law Applicable to Cyber Operations* (Cambridge: Cambridge University Press, 2017), p. 11.
2 Eric Talbot Jensen, "Cyber Sovereignty: The Way Ahead", *Texas International Law Journal* (2015), 50:2, p. 283.
3 Shawn M. Powers and Michael Jablonski, *The Real Cyber War: The Political Economy of Internet Freedom* (Chicago, IL: University of Illinois Press, 2015), p. 157.
4 Jensen (2015), p. 283.
5 Ibid, p. 284.
6 Powers and Jablonski (2015), p. 155.
7 The range of incidents that have occurred in the South China Sea are far too numerous to adequately source here. For the purposes of reader acquaintance with the issue, however, the Belfer Center's report will suffice as an introduction. Eleanor Freund, *Freedom of Navigation in the South China Sea: A Practical Guide* (June 2017). Available at www.belfercenter.org/publication/freedom-navigation-south-china-sea-practical-guide
8 Remarks by H.E. Xi Jinping, President of the People's Republic of China, at the Opening Ceremony of the Second World Internet Conference (16

December 2015). Available at www.fmprc.gov.cn/mfa_eng/wjdt_665385/zyjh_
665391/t1327570.shtml

9 Niels Nagelhus Schia and Lars Gjesvik, "China's Cyber Sovereignty", *Norwegian Institute of International Affairs, Policy Brief* (February 2017), p. 1.
10 Klimburg (2017), p. 255.
11 Schia and Gjesvik (2017), p. 1.
12 Gordon Corera, *Intercept: The Secret History of Computers and Spies* (London: Weidenfeld & Nicolson, 2016), p. 268.
13 James A. Lewis, "Sovereignty and the Role of Government in Cyberspace", *The Brown Journal of World Affairs* (Spring–Summer 2010), XVI:II, p. 63.
14 Jon R. Lindsay, "Introduction – China and Cybersecurity: Controversy and Context", in Jon R. Lindsay, Tai Ming Cheung and Derek S. Reveron (eds.), *China and Cybersecurity: Espionage, Strategy and Politics in the Digital Domain* (New York: Oxford University Press, 2015), p. 13.
15 Schia and Gjesvik (2017), p. 3.
16 Bruce Schneier, *Data and Goliath: The Hidden Battles to Collect Your Data and Control Your World* (New York: W.W. Norton, 2015), pp. 187–188.
17 Adam Segal, "When China Rules the Web", *Foreign Affairs* (September–October 2018), p. 10.
18 National Cyberspace Security Strategy (27 December 2016). Available at https://chinacopyrightandmedia.wordpress.com/2016/12/27/national-cyberspace-security-strategy/
19 Ibid.
20 Ibid.
21 Lindsay (2015), p. 11 (italics added).
22 Gordon Barrass and Nigel Inkster, "Xi Jinping: The Strategist Behind the Dream", *Survival* (2018), 60:1, p. 51.
23 National Cyberspace Security Strategy (2016).
24 French (2017), p. 660.
25 Michael Pillsbury, *The Hundred Year Marathon: China's Secret Strategy to Replace America as the Global Superpower* (New York: Henry Holt and Company, 2014), p. 207.
26 Ibid, p. 222.
27 National Cyberspace Security Strategy (2016).
28 Ibid.
29 Ibid.
30 Jack Margolin, *Russia, China, and the Push for 'Digital Sovereignty'* (2 December 2016). Available at https://theglobalobservatory.org/2016/12/russia-china-digital-sovereignty-shanghai-cooperation-organization/
31 Pasha Sharikov, *Understanding the Russian Approach to Information Security* (16 January 2018). Available at www.europeanleadershipnetwork.org/commentary/understanding-the-russian-approach-to-information-security/
32 Ibid.
33 Sara Moore, "Russia Country Profile", *Anomali Intelligence* (August 2017), p. 2. Available at https://dsimg.ubm-us.net/envelope/393193/563233/Russia%20Country%20Profile.pdf
34 The Ministry of Foreign Affairs of the Russian Federation, *Convention on International Information Security* (22 October 2011). Available at www.mid.ru/en/foreign_policy/official_documents/-/asset_publisher/CptICkB6BZ29/content/id/191666

35 Ibid.
36 State System of Legal Information, Decree of the President of the Russian Federation No. 646 (5 December 2016) "On Approving the Doctrine of Information Security for the Russian Federation". Available at http://publication.pravo.gov.ru/Document/View/0001201612060002
37 Sergey Sukhankin, "Russia's New Information Security Doctrine: Fencing Russia from the 'Outside World'", *Eurasia Daily Monitor* (2016), 13:198. Available at https://jamestown.org/program/russias-new-information-security-doctrine-fencing-russia-outside-world/
38 Ibid.
39 Klimburg (2017), p. 213.
40 Ibid, p. 222.
41 Paul R. Burgman, Jr., "Securing Cyberspace: China Leading the Way in Cyber Sovereignty", *The Diplomat* (18 May 2016). Available at https://thediplomat.com/2016/05/securing-cyberspace-china-leading-the-way-in-cyber-sovereignty/
42 Nick Lyall, "Cyber Sovereignty: The Sino-Russian Authoritarian Model", *Foreign Brief* (15 September 2017). Available at www.foreignbrief.com/tech-society/cyber-sovereignty-sino-russian-authoritarian-model/
43 Nigel Inkster, *China's Cyber Power* (London: IISS, 2016), p. 150.
44 Schia and Gjesvik (2017), p. 3.
45 Yuxi Wei, *China-Russia Cybersecurity Cooperation: Working Towards Cyber-Sovereignty* (21 June 2016). Available at https://jsis.washington.edu/news/china-russia-cybersecurity-cooperation-working-towards-cyber-sovereignty/
46 Executive Office of the President of the United States, *International Strategy for Cyberspace: Prosperity, Security, and Openness in a Networked World* (2011), p. 9. Available at https://obamawhitehouse.archives.gov/sites/default/files/rss_viewer/internationalstrategy_cyberspace.pdf
47 Michael N. Schmitt (ed.), *Tallinn Manual on the International Law Applicable to Cyber Warfare* (Cambridge: Cambridge University Press, 2013), p. 15.
48 Michael N. Schmitt (ed.), *Tallinn Manual 2.0 on the International Law Applicable to Cyber Operations* (Cambridge: Cambridge University Press, 2017), p. 11.
49 Ibid.
50 *Tallinn Manual* (2013), p. 16.
51 *Tallinn Manual* 2.0 (2017), p. 12.
52 Ibid, p. 13 (italics added).
53 Ibid.
54 Ibid.
55 Ibid, p. 15 (italics added).
56 *Tallinn Manual* (2013), p. 18.
57 Ibid, p. 11.
58 Servers.global, *Meeting the Challenge of Data Localisation Laws* (30 November 2016). Available at www.servers.global/meeting-the-challenge-of-data-localization-laws/
59 Courtney Bowman, "Data Localisation Laws: An Emerging Global Trend", *Jurist* (6 January 2017). Available at www.jurist.org/commentary/2017/01/courtney-bowman-data-localization/
60 Business Insider, "Vietnam Cyber Law Will Guard Against Fake News, Terrorism – Security Ministry", *Reuters* (31 October 2018). Available at https://uk.reuters.com/article/uk-vietnam-socialmedia/vietnam-cyber-law-will-guard-against-fake-news-terrorism-security-ministry-idUKKCN1N512C

61 Vinay Kesari, "Data Localisation and the Danger of a 'Splinternet'", *Factor Daily* (26 July 2018). Available at https://factordaily.com/data-localisation-and-the-danger-of-splinternet/

62 "India's Misguided Move Towards Data Localisation", *Financial Times* (10 September 2018). Available at www.ft.com/content/92bb34a8-b4e5-11e8-bbc3-ccd7de085ffe

63 HMG, *Investigatory Powers Act 2016, Part 4 Retention of Communications Data*. Available at www.legislation.gov.uk/ukpga/2016/25/contents/enacted

64 Ibid, Part 6 Bulk Warrants & Part 7 Bulk Personal Dataset Warrants.

65 Ibid, Part 5 Equipment Interference.

66 The Federal Service for the Supervision of Communications, Information Technology, and Mass Media, Federal Law No. 242-FZ. Available at https://pd.rkn.gov.ru/authority/p146/p191/

67 Matthew Newton and Julia Summers, *Russian Data Localisation Laws: Enriching 'Security' and the Economy* (28 February 2018). Available at https://jsis.washington.edu/news/russian-data-localization-enriching-security-economy/

68 Bowman (2017).

69 Ingrid Lunden, "Russia says '*nyet*', Continues LinkedIn Block After It Refuses to Store Data in Russia", *TechCrunch* (7 March 2017). Available at https://techcrunch.com/2017/03/07/russia-says-nyet-continues-linkedin-block-after-it-refuses-to-store-data-in-russia/

70 The Federal Service for the Supervision of Communications, Information Technology, *LinkedIn Refused to Eliminate Violations of Russian Law* (7 March 2017). Available at https://rkn.gov.ru/news/rsoc/news43486.htm

71 Leonid Levin quoted by Ksenia Idrisova, "Explainer: What Is Russia's New VPN Law All About", *BBC Monitoring* (1 November 2017). Available at www.bbc.com/news/technology-41829726

72 Jack Wagner, "China's Cybersecurity Law: What You Need to Know", *The Diplomat* (1 June 2017). Available at https://thediplomat.com/2017/06/chinas-cybersecurity-law-what-you-need-to-know/

73 Ibid.

74 Carly Ramsey and Carl Wootliff, "China's Cybersecurity Law: The Impossibility of Compliance?" *Forbes* (29 May 2017). Available at www.forbes.com/sites/riskmap/2017/05/29/chinas-cyber-security-law-the-impossibility-of-compliance/#5ba10c53471c

75 Yuan Yang, "China's Cyber Security Law Rattles Multinationals", *The Financial Times* (30 May 2017). Available at www.ft.com/content/b302269c-44ff-11e7-8519-9f94ee97d996

76 Sherisse Pham, "Use iCloud in China? Prepare to Share Your Data with a State-Run Firm", *CNN Business* (11 January 2018). Available at https://money.cnn.com/2018/01/10/technology/apple-china-icloud/index.html

77 Sherisse Pham, "Apple Is Under Fire for Moving iCloud Data to China", *CNN Business* (28 February 2018). Available at https://money.cnn.com/2018/02/28/technology/apple-icloud-data-china/index.html

78 Laignee Barron, "Amnesty International Is Accusing Apple of Betraying Chinese iCloud Users", *Time* (22 March 2018). Available at http://time.com/5210315/amnesty-international-apple-chinese-icloud-users-china/

79 "Complete Transcript, Video of Apple's CEO Tim Cook's EU Privacy Speech", *Computer World* (24 October 2018). Available at www.computerworld.com/article/3315623/security/complete-transcript-video-of-apple-ceo-tim-cooks-eu-privacy-speech.html

80 "China Tells Carriers to Block Access to Personal VPNs by February", *Bloomberg News* (10 July 2018). Available at www.bloomberg.com/news/articles/2017-07-10/china-is-said-to-order-carriers-to-bar-personal-vpns-by-february

81 Benjamin Has, "China Moves to Block VPNs from 2018", *The Guardian* (11 July 2017). Available at www.theguardian.com/world/2017/jul/11/china-moves-to-block-internet-vpns-from-2018

82 Segal (2018), p. 12.

83 Olivia Solon, "China Cracks Down on VPNs, Making It Harder to Circumvent the Great Firewall", *The Guardian* (23 January 2017). Available at www.theguardian.com/technology/2017/jan/23/china-vpn-cleanup-great-firewall-censorship

84 Katherine Kendrick, "Data Localisation: Risky Business", *Forbes* (19 February 2015). Available at www.forbes.com/sites/realspin/2015/02/19/risky-business-data-localization/#474573751077

85 Viktor Mayer-Schonberger and Thomas Ramge, "A Big Choice for Big Tech", *Foreign Affairs* (September–October 2018).

86 Klimburg (2017), p. 16.

87 John Perry Barlow, *A Declaration on the Independence of Cyberspace* (8 February 1996). Available at www.eff.org/cyberspace-independence

88 Thomas Rid, *The Rise of the Machines: The Lost History of Cybernetics* (London: Scribe Publications, 2016), p. 255.

89 David Runciman, *How Democracy Ends* (London: Profile Books Ltd, 2018), p. 212.

90 A very effective summary of Gore's contribution can be found in Walter Isaacson, *The Innovators: How a Group of Hackers, Inventors, Geniuses and Geeks Created the Digital Revolution* (London: Simon & Schuster, 2014), pp. 400–403.

91 Karen Kornbluh, "The Internet's Lost Promise: And How America Can Restore It", *Foreign Affairs* (September–October 2018), p. 37.

92 William J. Drake, Vinton G. Cerf and Wolfgang Kleinwachter, *Internet Fragmentation: An Overview* (2016) World Economic Forum, Future of the Internet Initiative White Paper, p. 10. Available at www.weforum.org/reports/internet-fragmentation-an-overview

93 Tom Wheeler, *Keeping the Internet Open for the Future*, Brookings Institution (20 June 2017). Available at www.brookings.edu/blog/techtank/2017/06/20/keeping-the-internet-open-for-the-future/

94 FCC, *Restoring Internet Freedom Order* (11 June 2018). Available at https://docs.fcc.gov/public/attachments/DOC-351481A1.pdf

95 Via an addition made to Article 19 of the Universal Declaration of Human Rights. Catherine Howell and Darrell M. West, *The Internet as a Human Right*, Brookings Institution (7 November 2016). Available at www.brookings.edu/blog/techtank/2016/11/07/the-internet-as-a-human-right/

96 Olesya Tkacheva, Lowell H. Schwartz, Martin C. Libicki, Julie E. Taylor, Jeffrey Martini, and Caroline Baxter, *Internet Freedom and Political Space* (Santa Monica, CA: RAND, 2013), pp. 432–433.

97 British Foreign Secretary William Hague, *Security and Freedom in the Cyber Age – Finding the Rules of the Road* (4 February 2011). Available at www.gov.uk/government/speeches/security-and-freedom-in-the-cyber-age-seeking-the-rules-of-the-road

98 HMG, *The UK Cyber Security Strategy: Protecting and Promoting the UK in a Digital World* (London: HMSO, 2011), p. 21. Available at www.gov.uk/government/publications/cyber-security-strategy

99 Eneken Tikk, "Introduction", in Zine Homburger, Liisi Adamson and Els de Busser (eds.), *Voluntary, Non-Binding Norms for Responsible State Behaviour in the Use of Information and Telecommunications Technology: A Commentary* (2017), pp. 2–4. Available at www.un.org/disarmament/publications/civilsociety/civil-society-and-disarmament-2017/

100 Michele Markoff quoted in Owen Bowcott, "Dispute Along Cold War Lines Leads to Collapse of UN Cyberwarfare Talks", *The Guardian* (23 August 2017). Available at www.theguardian.com/world/2017/aug/23/uncyberwarfare-negotiations-collapsed-in-june-it-emerges

101 Elaine Korzak, "UN GGE on Cybersecurity: The End of an Era", *The Diplomat* (31 July 2017). Available at https://thediplomat.com/2017/07/un-gge-on-cybersecurity-have-china-and-russia-just-made-cyberspace-less-safe/

102 Alex Grigsby, "The Year in Review: The Death of the UN GGE Process?" *Council on Foreign Relations* (21 December 2017). Available at www.cfr.org/blog/year-review-death-un-gge-process

103 Korzak (2017).

104 Klimburg (2017), p. 17.

105 Henry Kissinger, *World Order: Reflections on the Character of Nations and the Course of History* (New York: Penguin Books, 2015), pp. 456–457.

106 Alexander Hamilton, Federalist No. 1 General Introduction (27 October 1787), within *The US Constitution and Other Key American Writings* (San Diego, CA: Word Cloud Classics, 2015), p. 51.

107 Jean-Jacques Rousseau, *A Treatise on the Social Compact: Or the Principles of Politic Law* (Oxford: Oxford University Press, 1764), p. 37.

108 Benjamin Wittes and Gabriella Blum, *The Future of Violence: Robots and Germs, Hackers and Drones* (New York: Basic Books, 2015), p. 263.

109 Ibid, p. 274.

110 William Beveridge, *Why I am a Liberal* (London: Herbert Jenkins, 1945), p. 9.

111 Yochai Benkler, *The Wealth of Networks: How Social Production Transforms Markets and Freedom* (New Haven: Yale University Press, 2006), p. 103.

112 Ibid.

113 John J. Mearshimer, *The Great Delusion: Liberal Dreams and International Realities* (New Haven: Yale University Press, 2018), p. 21.

114 Ibid, p. 11.

115 Ibid, p. 164.

116 Graham Allison, "The Myth of the Liberal Order", *Foreign Affairs* (July–August 2018). Available at www.foreignaffairs.com/articles/2018-06-14/myth-liberal-order

117 National Security Council, *NSC-68: United States Objectives and Programs for National Security* (14 April 1950), p. 64. Available at www.trumanlibrary.org/whistlestop/study_collections/coldwar/documents/pdf/10-1.pdf

118 Allison (2018).

119 Daniel Fried and Alina Polyakova, "Democratic Defense Against Disinformation", *The Atlantic Council* (February 2018), p. 3. Available at www.atlanticcouncil.org/publications/reports/democratic-defense-against-disinformation

120 Michael J. Mazarr, "The Real History of the Liberal Order: Neither Myth Nor Accident", *Foreign Affairs* (7 August 2018). Available at www.foreignaffairs.com/articles/2018-08-07/real-history-liberal-order

121 Eliana Johnson, "Why Trump Hasn't Fired Mattis", *Politico* (23 March 2018). Available at www.politico.com/magazine/story/2018/03/23/james-mattis-defense-secretary-how-to-succeed-in-trump-cabinet-without-getting-fired-217699

122 Statement to the General Assembly by Foreign Minister Meir (1 March 1957). Available at www.mfa.gov.il/mfa/foreignpolicy/mfadocuments/yearbook1/pages/26%20statement%20to%20the%20general%20assembly%20by%20foreign%20mi.aspx

123 Pamela Engel, "Obama Reportedly Declined to Enforce Red Line in Syria After Iran Threatened to Back Out of Nuclear Deal", *Business Insider* (23 August 2016). Available at http://uk.businessinsider.com/obama-red-line-syria-iran-2016-8?r=US&IR=T

124 PMs speech to the Lord Mayor's Banquet (13 November 2017). Available at www.gov.uk/government/speeches/pm-speech-to-the-lord-mayors-banquet-2017

125 John Stuart Mill, *Littell's Living Ages (Inaugural Address at University of St. Andrews: 01/02/1867) Number 1189, Fourth Series* (Boston, MA: Littell and Gay, 1867), p. 664.

126 Bernard Brodie, *War and Politics* (London: Cassell & Co. Ltd, 1974), p. 452.

127 Patrick J. Deneen, *Why Liberalism Failed* (New Haven: Yale University Press, 2018), p. 231.

128 Yascha Mounk, *The People vs. Democracy: Why Our Freedom Is in Danger and How to Save It* (Cambridge, MA: Harvard University Press, 2018), p. 25 (italics original).

129 Botsman (2017), p. 445.

130 Snyder (2018), p. 525 (italics added).

131 Kornbluh (2018), p. 33.

132 Michele Flournoy and Michael Sulmeyer, "Battlefield Internet: A Plan for Securing Cyberspace", *Foreign Affairs* (September–October 2018), p. 40.

133 Yuval Noah Harari, "Why Technology Favours Tyranny", *The Atlantic* (October 2018), 322:3, p. 64.

Conclusion
The battle for the soul of the Internet

Previously, this author argued that the attempt to make strategic sense of cyberspace was plagued by uncertainty and that it would take time for any kind of 'strategic clarity' to emerge.[1] The rate of acceleration that events alone – without consideration of technological advancement – have brought into the world of cyberspace has certainly left such a view well in the rear view mirror. Uncertainty no doubt still exists, but it can be argued to exist as a purposely strategic application of cyber methods, one that as seen through the 2016 presidential election in the United States has been precisely to sow discord and confusion and even erode the faith of the electorate in democracy itself. And Russian employment of cyber methods across Ukraine and beyond have demonstrated two important truths, first that 'any new technology may find strategic employment'[2] and second, 'Autocrats know how to use tech, too.'[3] What now exists in no uncertain terms is a new canon of experience with which to base more far-ranging assessments and an emerging understanding that conflict in, about, and through cyberspace appears quite different to what was originally thought.[4]

The sheer range of events to cover in any assessment and analysis has become truly astounding in such a short space of time this decade. This can be seen through events ranging from Operation Aurora to Stuxnet, the Conficker criminal wave to the global cyber attacks of WannaCry and Not-Petya that paralysed entire health services and costs billions of dollars to major corporations. Then there remains the relentless campaigns of cyber espionage against the West with targets as diverse as NASA to university campuses, which former NSA Director Keith Alexander labels as constituting 'the greatest transfer of wealth in history.'[5] Further to this is a realisation that we 'now seem a long way from the Arab Spring in 2011, when social media seemed to give democracy activists an advantage'[6] and proven the liberating democratic force of the Internet. That view has given way to fears precipitated by the Russian election interference in 2016 of authoritarian use of technology to fracture the democratic process itself, corroding the faith of the people from within by magnifying our worst fears and prejudices through social media echo chambers spouting hateful fake news in horrifying volumes.

This work has sought to establish what circumstances led to this state of affairs in cyber security by revealing the insecurities suffered in and through cyberspace, reflecting challenges that run far deeper than the immediate impacts of cybercrime, cyber espionage, or cyber attacks themselves. Instead, it needs to be accepted that the maturation of computing technologies, connected with internetworking innovations and encryption practices, have presented fundamental disruptions to social, economic, and political orders themselves. In a similar vein to how the security impact of the railway as part of the Industrial Revolution ran far deeper than how armies mobilised and fought, so too is the impact of cyberspace about far more than applications by the NSA or military forces worldwide. Accepting this reality is key to being able to begin answering the second question this work tackled, where might we be going with the solutions on offer?

With that broadened impact in mind, a series of conclusions are offered on the politics and technology of cyber security:

1. There are technological realities that greatly shape our security concerns

It was stated early in this work that much theorising on cyberspace to date betrayed a significant weakness among scholars from social science, humanities, and legal backgrounds – being ill-informed as to the technological realities underpinning cyberspace itself. It can hardly be seen as coincidental that the culture of hyperbolic theorising on all things cyber was speculative rather than underwritten by a solid understanding of what was and was not possible within technological parameters. Gray notes well that technology has its own habit of fuelling scholarly assumptions, leading to either technophilia or technophobia,[7] as has been regularly seen with all things cyber. This is why a level of analytic empathy is required with comparisons of cyber security to the early air power theorists, who so too issued technophilic prophecies about air power's potency that well endured throughout the twentieth century, even when faced with contradictory evidence in reality.[8]

Due to what can only be described as the poverty of technological understanding across the social sciences, humanities, and law departments in universities, there is a need for a technological "toolkit" that this work has provided with its exploration of cyberspace's underlying technologies. A common denominator is needed and provided that does not claim to be technically exhaustive – it most certainly is not, and far deeper technical edification is needed for those seeking careers in operational cyber security – but is argued as being comprehensive in providing scholars and students from non-technical backgrounds with the key elements they need to discuss cyber security with technical accuracy. Once such rigour is applied to the core technologies as has been attempted here, three conditioning realities become apparent that will shape the interaction between technological possibilities and political desires.

The first of these is that *there will be an increased tension between the universality of Internet standards and the demands of political sovereignty*. In particular, the reliance of communications and the global economy on TCP/IP and DNS through the root server will ensure the tension between maintaining the globally connected Internet based on universal protocols and satisfying political demands to impose sovereignty will only increase, or certainly encounter difficult episodes in practice. Serious propositions for fragmentation would involve either wholesale segregation from the global networks in the fashion of North Korea, or the implementation of new technologies that permit leaving the original infrastructure behind. This is an important factor to consider for, as was noted by the Global Commission on Internet Governance, 'efforts to gain political and economic advantage bring the network toward fragmentation and away from universality.'[9] And although this author accepts the views of Drake, Cerf, and Kleinwachter in tempering the debate on the doubtful likelihood of full-scale fragmentations,[10] it does need to be accepted that political desires to assert sovereignty are increasingly at odds with the technical engineering views of the desirability of *increased* universality. In accepting this conditioning reality and its interaction with the concerns of political actors, far more credence is lent to Khanna's view that 'geopolitical competition is evolving from war over territory to war over connectivity.'[11] The reassertion of politics over this space is still feeling out the contours of the technology's limits and vulnerabilities and trying to match them with political vision.

Second, *geography still matters*.[12] Among the many utopian visions projected into cyberspace has long been an assertion that geography was no longer relevant, that a demise of geographic importance[13] was a self-evident reality in our modern hyper-connected, globalised world. Yet with the importance of submarine cables and data centres established in this work, it is plain that cyberspace has a fundamentally physical reality that is grounded in the geographically real world. Internet protocols cannot function without cables to travel through, and data must ultimately be stored somewhere physically real. These two technological facts carry significant conditioning realities of great interest to strategic actors: first, who owns the infrastructure? A significant geopolitical advantage underwrote the ability of the NSA and GCHQ to conduct the surveillance operations that were betrayed by Edward Snowden.

That advantage was dominance of the submarine cable infrastructure through which a disproportionate amount of traffic traversed. This 'shape and structure of the internet'[14] where cables traverse, land, and what percentage of global traffic they carry is a prized geopolitical advantage that the Snowden revelations severely compromised for the United States and United Kingdom, in ways that may yet take many years to fully manifest. In addition to the question of infrastructure are the numerous attempts at data localisation laws worldwide; if the data one seeks can be stored within one's sovereign territory, one can assert legal jurisdiction over it.

Finally, *the proliferation of encryption* will shape security concerns greatly. Almost, though not quite, regardless of whether there are fundamental fragmentations in Internet infrastructure, or of whom underlying infrastructure is owned by, access to encryption will continue to present challenges especially to the effective exercise of sovereignty over cyberspace. The ability for politically motivated individuals to prepare and launch terrorist attacks, for large criminal enterprises to be sustained online, through to hundreds of other applications behind encryption pose great challenges to the state's ability to deliver security and the rule of law to individuals. When readers acknowledge the difficulty for authorities in London to anticipate the Westminster attack against Parliament in 2017, due in large part to the end-to-end encryption offered by WhatsApp, a larger degree of empathy can be given to the American view of the 1990s when the NSA lost their "crypto-war" against those who sought to stop encryption being classified as a weapons class.

Rid is very fair in assessing that the crypto-anarchy movement had a mixed record of success against the US government, yet they did achieve two significant milestones that helped shape the future of encryption's place in the development of cyberspace to come. In the first, the court cases by Daniel Bernstein in the 1990s led to recognition in US law that 'software code was constitutionally protected speech, eventually ushering in the end of the hated cryptographic expos control regime.'[15] Their other achievement was ideological, spreading the belief that crypto technologies themselves were libertarian at heart, and that their spread would only be for the betterment of individual liberties.[16] Where the position of liberal democratic states especially falls on the place of encryption will be a key development of the vision offered by Free Internet Coalition, for the role that encryption plays will represent a significant foundation of maintaining trust in future cyberspace. The temptation for democratic states will be to regress back to a view that sees encryption as a threat, when in the creation of any sort of revised social contract for the digital age the reality might need to be accepted that encryption may well play a central role at the heart of protecting civil liberties.

2. The apolitical honeymoon is over; political sovereignty will be established

This work has devoted considerable effort to establishing what seemingly appeared to be unacknowledged historical context of the Internet's apolitical infancy. The 1990s heyday of liberal triumphalism provided the Internet with a precious incubator that allowed it to safely grow away from significant political challenge from without. This is true even notwithstanding the Russian success at solidifying information security as an item on the United Nations agenda from 1998, which was not enough to check the explosion of the Open Internet in aggressively liberal fashion across the world.

Despite these origins, 'Cyberspace does not exist independent of politics,'[17] and sovereign nation states now recognise the importance of cyberspace and have generated competing visions for what the future of cyberspace should look like. The 'sovereignty gap'[18] that Kello rightly identified where state influence – even its fundamental importance – has waned is certainly now the subject of vigorous redress from governments all over the world. Data localisation laws are the clearest shared measure between democratic and authoritarian states who are seeking to impose an asymmetric measure against the virtual world to enable the assertion of sovereign authority. Then there are far more extreme measures not shared between nations, with China's Social Credit System so far representing the far end of the spectrum. In this regard, Klimburg's view is best in asserting that should the Chinese project be successful, it will represent the embryonic form of how the web would darken in the most fearful sense to anybody with a liberal mindset.[19]

It is certainly now a high priority for nation states to close the sovereignty gap and establish rightful authority over a space that, although never *un*governed, has developed in ways that were never expected. Perhaps the biggest challenge facing the Free Internet Coalition is recognising that they have never viewed the contest as a geopolitical one, whereas Beijing, Moscow, and others have always viewed the Internet as a threat to their national security.[20] Those states among the Western democracies need to recognise that the 'Code War,' as Carlin labels it, 'has already begun.'[21]

The incessant presence of cybercrime, cyber espionage, and innovations in how to apply cyber attacks against nations have contributed to the motivations as to why nation states need to assert sovereign authority over this space. The continued development of technology will of course shape the contours of what is technically possible and should also challenge what is political desirable, which should lead to debates in the public interest. What is also therefore crucial is that the Free Internet Coalition begins to see that accepting the necessity of sovereignty is not the same as accepting the position of the Cyber Sovereignty movement. With this in mind, Carlin is also right to note that 'a high-level societal commitment' akin to a 'Cyber Moonshot or a Cyber Manhattan Project'[22] is needed. Where this author differs to Carlin, however, is to challenge his view that such a project should be a purely technical engineering challenge to create a more secure future cyberspace than we have at present. This author's view is that such a project should be focused as much, if not more so, on the political position held by the individual in future cyberspace.

The state must not only establish sovereignty over cyberspace, it must also legitimise its position of authority in a space that has potentially challenged the long-term relevance of the nation state concept itself. No notion of authority can exist in a liberal democratic society without the explicit consent and blessing of its electorate; to do so in cyberspace while fundamentally redressing the balance of individual insecurity online requires a revision of the social contract as it exists with citizens. Powers and Jablonski note this problem well in their conclusion, in stating this issue of legitimate state authority is a 'stagnant area' of academic inquiry.[23] The big project that Carlin envisages should benefit not only from continued scientific and engineering innovations, but also from renewed and reenergised public debate about what balance of civil liberties the individual should enjoy online, where the boundaries of privacy blur, as well as what societal expectations are placed on behaviour. Discussions on the place of sovereignty in cyberspace have been entirely skewed towards the state so far; the vision of the Free Internet Coalition cannot make headway without significant energy being devoted once more towards redefining what the liberty of the individual means in a digital age.

3. Cyberspace must be seen as a crucial geopolitical battleground of the 21st century

While caution must always be taken with extreme, near-dystopian prophecies such as Klimburg's darkening web, it must indeed be recognised that the 'battle for the soul of the Internet,'[24] as Inkster labels it, is well underway and extends far further than debates about the next clever military application or the next global cyber criminal attack. Instead, the *'unpeace'*[25] that Kello identifies captures well the dynamic of intense geopolitical rivalry that has been building in cyberspace, yet fails to reach the existential proportions worthy of being labelled a new Cold War. Despite not reaching the heights of concern of the Cold War, this work hopes to have shown that the importance of cyberspace will carry disproportionate results to the development of geopolitics in the twenty-first century.

That this is so is because whichever vision ultimately succeeds – Cyber Sovereignty or the Free Internet Coalition – will both greatly consolidate their own political authority as well as derive significant strategic advantage internationally in the development of the multi-polar order. Were Cyber Sovereignty to prevail and succeed in dividing the democratic nations into an acceptance that the state should enjoy near-absolute sovereign status, a future of fractured Internets should be accepted where it is difficult to even know what is occurring behind the borders of nations like Russia and China. Klimburg's darkening web would come courtesy of a "digital iron curtain" falling over large segments of the world's population, protecting authoritarian regimes not only from external interference, but also even from the possibility of their citizens being provided with information deemed unsuitable.

For the Free Internet Coalition to succeed, a great many things need to happen that were detailed in the previous chapter. Success cannot, however, be seen purely as a repeat of the liberal triumphalism that accompanied the end of the Cold War; indeed, such triumphalism contributed to the rooting of the significant insecurities that are today faced throughout cyberspace. Instead, success for the Free Internet Coalition must be seen as a more nuanced and ambitious project that would include the achievement of the five aforementioned objectives: a revision of the social contract; an acceptance of other political positions, ideally with a nuanced acceptance of sovereignty in cyberspace that does not yield to the Cyber Sovereignty view; a focus on the unity of democratic allies behind a common vision akin to that achieved in the Cold War; the declaration of red lines in order to establish what is not tolerable to the liberal order; and the challenge of bad behaviour that goes beyond mere rhetoric and carries actual punitive measures on transgressors. Above all, the effort must highlight and not abandon core liberal values of openness, freedom of expression, and liberty[26] as part of long-term struggle to shape cyberspace in the liberal vision.

How this battle for the soul of the Internet develops will be a crucial determinant of twenty-first century geopolitics, for which political vision dominates the greatest channel for information flows the world has ever seen will go far in shaping our reality, both perceived and actual. Our perceived reality is already incessantly shaped by algorithms that are increasingly seen as inherently biased at best, but deliberately biased at worst; there is no reason at all to think that this situation will abate; in fact, it can only be forecast to accelerate now that methods at manipulating reality and attacking truth have been proven in their potency. Our actual reality has been shaped by the ownership of Internet architectures and the contest to establish rightful political authority over a space that has so far eluded it; Khanna should be taken seriously with his vision that geopolitics in this century will be played out 'in the matrix of physical and digital infrastructure.'[27] Success for either political vision will also go far in answering the fundamental question of what political order best suits the twenty-first century multi-polar order, authoritarianism or democracy? Harari is persuasive in arguing that liberalism so far is losing credibility due to its inability to provide for its societies, and that the core weakness behind the Soviet Union's demise – the inefficiency of its centralised state system – may be provided with a renewed ability with artificial intelligence.[28] Should these fears be proven true and should Cyber Sovereignty gain further traction, the simple question as put by Larson may well take on a very serious following indeed: 'Who needs democracy when you have data?'[29]

Notes

1 Danny Steed, "The Strategic Implications of Cyber Warfare", in James Andrew Green (ed.), *Cyber Warfare: A Multidisciplinary Analysis* (Abingdon: Routledge, 2015), p. 92.
2 Colin S. Gray, *Theory of Strategy* (Oxford: Oxford University Press, 2018), p. 105.
3 Larry Diamond in Thomas Carothers, "Why Technology Hasn't Delivered More Democracy", *Foreign Policy* (3 June 2015). Available at https://foreignpolicy.com/2015/06/03/why-technology-hasnt-delivered-more-democracy-democratic-transition/
4 Neal Pollard and Matthew G. Devost, "Is Cyberwar Turning Out to Be Very Different from What We Thought?" *Politico* (6 August 2016). Available at www.politico.com/magazine/story/2016/08/is-cyberwar-turning-out-to-be-very-different-from-what-we-thought-214136
5 Josh Rogin, "NSA Chief: Cybercrime Constitute 'the greatest transfer of wealth in history'", *Foreign Policy* (12 July 2012). Available at https://foreignpolicy.com/2012/07/09/nsa-chief-cybercrime-constitutes-the-greatest-transfer-of-wealth-in-history/
6 Moises Naim and Philip Bennett, "The Anti-Information Age", *The Atlantic* (16 February 2015). Available at www.theatlantic.com/international/archive/2015/02/government-censorship-21st-century-internet/385528/
7 Colin S. Gray, *Perspectives on Strategy* (Oxford: Oxford University Press, 2013), p. 156.
8 David Betz, "Cyberpower in Strategic Affairs: Neither Unthinkable Nor Blessed", *Journal of Strategic Studies* (2012), 35:5, pp. 692–694.
9 Laura Denardis, *One Internet: An Evidentiary Basis for Policy Making on Internet Universality and Fragmentation* (July 2016), Global Commission on Internet Governance, Paper Series No. 38, p. 10.
10 William J. Drake, Vinton G. Cerf and Wolfgang Kleinwachter, *Internet Fragmentation: An Overview* (2016) World Economic Forum, Future of the Internet Initiative White Paper, pp. 3–6. Available at www.weforum.org/reports/internet-fragmentation-an-overview
11 Khanna (2016), pp. 27–28.
12 This author stands by this conclusion reached in a previous work. Steed in Green (ed.) (2016), pp. 87–89.
13 Murray is but one example in a range of literature that hailed such a demise. W.E. Murray, *Geographies of Globalisation* (Abingdon: Routledge, 2006), Ch. 1.

14 Adam Segal, *The Hacked World Order: How Nations Fight, Trade, Manoeuvre and Manipulate in the Digital Age* (New York: Public Affairs, 2016), p. 62.
15 Rid (2016), p. 276.
16 Ibid, p. 292.
17 Segal (2016), p. 58.
18 Kello (2017), p. 254.
19 Klimburg (2017), pp. 258–259.
20 Segal (2016), p. 361.
21 John P. Carlin, *Dawn of the Code War: America's Battle Against Russia, China, and the Rising Global Cyber Threat* (New York: Public Affairs, 2018), p. 709.
22 Ibid, p. 568.
23 Shawn M. Powers and Michael Jablonski, *The Real Cyber War: The Political Economy of Internet Freedom* (Urbana, Chicago, IL: University of Illinois Press, 2015), p. 208.
24 Nigel Inkster, *China's Cyber Power* (London: IISS, 2016), Ch. 4.
25 Kello (2017), p. 249.
26 As sagely concluded in Alina Polyakova and Spencer P. Boyer, *The Future of Political Warfare: Russia, the West, and the Coming Age of Global Digital Competition* (March 2018) The Brookings Institute, p. 18. Available at www.brookings.edu/research/the-future-of-political-warfare-russia-the-west-and-the-coming-age-of-global-digital-competition/
27 Khanna (2016), pp. 28–29.
28 Yuval Noah Harari, "Why Technology Favours Tyranny", *The Atlantic* (October 2018), 322:2, p. 68.
29 Christina Larson, "Who Needs Democracy When You Have Data?" *MIT Technology Review* (September–October 2018), 121:5.

Bibliography

Articles

Allen, T. S. and Moore, A. J., "Victory Without Casualties: Russia's Information Operations", *Parameters* (Spring 2018), 48:1

Allison, Graham, "The Myth of the Liberal Order", *Foreign Affairs* (July–August 2018). Available at www.foreignaffairs.com/articles/2018-06-14/myth-liberal-order

Barrass, Gordon, and Inkster, Nigel, "Xi Jinping: The Strategist Behind the Dream", *Survival* (2018), 60:1

Barron, Laignee, "Amnesty International Is Accusing Apple of Betraying Chinese iCloud Users", *Time* (22 March 2018). Available at http://time.com/5210315/amnesty-international-apple-chinese-icloud-users-china/

Betz, David, "Cyberpower in Strategic Affairs: Neither Unthinkable Nor Blessed", *Journal of Strategic Studies* (2012), 35:5

Burgman Jr. Paul R., "Securing Cyberspace: China Leading the Way in Cyber Sovereignty", *The Diplomat* (18 May 2016). Available at https://thediplomat.com/2016/05/securing-cyberspace-china-leading-the-way-in-cyber-sovereignty/

Carothers, Thomas, "Why Technology Hasn't Delivered More Democracy", *Foreign Policy* (03 June 2015). Available at https://foreignpolicy.com/2015/06/03/why-technology-hasnt-delivered-more-democracy-democratic-transition/

Cassidy, John, "Lessons from Apple vs the FBI", *The New Yorker* (29 March 2016). Available at www.newyorker.com/news/john-cassidy/lessons-from-apple-versus-the-f-b-i

The Economist, "Tim Cook, Privacy Martyr?" (20 February 2016). Available at www.economist.com/business/2016/02/20/tim-cook-privacy-martyr

The Economist, "My Truth Against Yours", The Future of War Special Report (27 January–2 February 2018)

The Economist, "Sailing the Wired Seas" (10 March 2018). Available at www.economist.com/technology-quarterly/2018/03/10/sailing-the-wired-seas

Flournoy, Michele, and Sulmeyer, Michael, "Battlefield Internet: A Plan for Securing Cyberspace", *Foreign Affairs* (September–October 2018)

Harari, Yuval Noah, "Why Technology Favours Tyranny", *The Atlantic* (October 2018), 322:3

Johnson, Eliana, "Why Trump Hasn't Fired Mattis", *Politico* (23 March 2018). Available at www.politico.com/magazine/story/2018/03/23/james-mattis-defense-secretary-how-to-succeed-in-trump-cabinet-without-getting-fired-217699

Kornbluh, Karen, "The Internet's Lost Promise: And How America Can Restore It", *Foreign Affairs* (September–October 2018)

Korzak, Elaine, "UN GGE on Cybersecurity: The End of an Era", *The Diplomat* (31 July 2017). Available at https://thediplomat.com/2017/07/un-gge-on-cybersecurity-have-china-and-russia-just-made-cyberspace-less-safe/

Larson, Christina, "Who Needs Democracy When You Have Data?" *MIT Technology Review* (September–October 2018), 121:5

Lewis, James A., "Sovereignty and the Role of the Government in Cyberspace", *Brown Journal of World Affairs* (Spring–Summer 2010), XVI:II, p. 58

Limnell, Jarno, "The Exploitation of Cyber Domain as Part of Warfare: Russo-Ukrainian War", *International Journal of Cyber-Security and Digital Forensics* (2015), 4:4

Lindsey, Richard A., "What the Arab Spring Tells Us About the Future of Social Media in Revolutionary Movements", *Small Wars Journal* (2013). Available at http://smallwarsjournal.com/jrnl/art/what-the-arab-spring-tells-us-about-the-future-of-social-media-in-revolutionary-movements

Lyall, Nick, "Cyber Sovereignty: The Sino-Russian Authoritarian Model", *Foreign Brief* (15 September 2017). Available at www.foreignbrief.com/tech-society/cyber-sovereignty-sino-russian-authoritarian-model/

Mayer-Schonberger, Viktor, and Ramge, Thomas, "A Big Choice for Big Tech", *Foreign Affairs* (September–October 2018)

Mazarr, Michael J., "The Real History of the Liberal Order: Neither Myth Nor Accident", *Foreign Affairs* (7 August 2018). Available at www.foreignaffairs.com/articles/2018-08-07/real-history-liberal-order

Meyer, Jane, "How Russia Helped Swing the Election for Trump", *The New Yorker* (1 October 2018). Available at www.newyorker.com/magazine/2018/10/01/how-russia-helped-to-swing-the-election-for-trump

Naim, Moises, and Bennett, Philip, "The Anti-Information Age", *The Atlantic* (16 February 2015). Available at www.theatlantic.com/international/archive/2015/02/government-censorship-21st-century-internet/385528/

Piore, Adam, "No, Big Tech Didn't Make Us Polarised (But It Sure Helps)", *MIT Technology Review* (September–October 2018), 121:5

Pollard, Neal, and Devost, Matthew G., "Is Cyberwar Turning Out to Be Very Different from What We Thought?" *Politico* (6 August 2016). Available at www.politico.com/magazine/story/2016/08/is-cyberwar-turning-out-to-be-very-different-from-what-we-thought-214136

Raustiala, Kal, "An Internet Whole and Free: Why Washington Was Right to Give Up Control", *Foreign Affairs* (March–April 2017), 96:2

Segal, Adam, "When China Rules the Web", *Foreign Affairs* (September–October 2018)

Steed, Danny, "Cyber Power and Strategy – So What?" *Infinity Journal* (Spring 2011), 1

Sukhankin, Sergey, "Russia's New Information Security Doctrine: Fencing Russia from the 'Outside World'", *Eurasia Daily Monitor* (2016), 13:198. Available at https://jamestown.org/program/russias-new-information-security-doctrine-fencing-russia-outside-world/

Talbot Jensen, Eric, "Cyber Sovereignty: The Way Ahead", *Texas International Law Journal* (2015), 50:2

Waddell, Kaveh, "Does Russia's Election Hacking Signal a New Era in Espionage?" *The Atlantic* (15 December 2016). Available at www.theatlantic.com/technology/archive/2016/12/russias-election-meddling-was-an-intelligence-coup/510743/

Wagner, Jack, "China's Cybersecurity Law: What You Need to Know", *The Diplomat* (1 June 2017). Available at https://thediplomat.com/2017/06/chinas-cyber-security-law-what-you-need-to-know/

Yannakogeorgos, Panayotis A., "Internet Governance and National Security", *Strategic Studies Quarterly* (Fall 2012)

Books

Andrew, Christopher, *The Secret World: A History of Intelligence* (London: Allen Lane, 2018)

Arquilla, John, and Ronfeldt, David (eds.), *In Athena's Camp: Preparing for Conflict in the Information Age* (Santa Monica, CA: RAND, 1997)

Bacevich, Andrew J., *American Empire: The Realities and Consequences of US Diplomacy* (Cambridge, MA: Harvard University Press, 2004)

Bartlett, Jamie, *Radicals Chasing Utopia: Inside the Rogue Movements Trying to Change the World* (New York: Nation Books, 2017)

Belfiore, Michael, *The Department of Mad Scientists: How DARPA Is Remaking Our World, from the Internet to Artificial Limbs* (London: Harper Collins eBooks, 2010)

Benkler, Yochai, *The Wealth of Networks: How Social Production Transforms Markets and Freedom* (New Haven: Yale University Press, 2006)

Beveridge, William, *Why I am a Liberal* (London: Herbert Jenkins, 1945)

Black, Jeremy, *The Power of Knowledge: How Information and Technology Made the Modern World* (London: Yale University Press, 2014)

Blum, Andrew, *Tubes: A Journey to the Centre of the Internet* (New York: Harper Collins, 2012)

Bobbitt, Philip, *The Shield of Achilles: War, Peace and the Course of History* (London: Penguin Books, 2002)

Botsman, Rachel, *Who Can You Trust: How Technology Brought Us Together and Why It Might Drive Us Apart* (New York: Public Affairs, 2017)

Brendon, Piers, *The Decline and Fall of the British Empire, 1781–1997* (New York: Alfred A. Knopf, 2008)

Brodie, Bernard, *War and Politics* (London: Cassell & Co. Ltd, 1974)

Brzezinski, Zbigniew, *Strategic Vision: America and the Crisis of Global Power* (New York: Basic Books, 2012)

Burke, Jason, *The 9/11 Wars* (London: Penguin Books, 2012)

Buzan, Barry, and Hansen, Lene (eds.), *International Security Volume II: The Transition to the Post-Cold War Security Agenda* (Los Angeles, CA: Sage Publications Ltd., 2007)

Cairncross, Frances, *The Death of Distance: How the Communications Revolution Is Changing Our Lives* 2nd Ed. (London: Texere Publishing Limited, 2001)

Carlin, John P., *The Code War: America's Battle Against Russia, China, and the Rising Global Cyber Threat* (New York: Public Affairs, 2018)

Clarke, Richard A., and Knake, Robert K., *Cyber War: The Next Threat to National Security and What to Do About It* (New York: Harper Collins, 2012)

Comey, James, *A Higher Loyalty: Truth, Lies, and Leadership* (London: Macmillan, 2018)

Corera, Gordon, *Intercept: The Secret History of Computers and Spies* (London: Weidenfeld & Nicolson, 2016)

Darwin, John, *The Empire Project: The Rise and Fall of the British World System, 1830–1970* (Cambridge: Cambridge University Press, 2009)

Deneen, Patrick J., *Why Liberalism Failed* (New Haven: Yale University Press, 2018)

Dunn Cavelty, Myriam, Mauer, Victor, and Krishna-Hensel, Sani Felicia (eds.), *Power and Security in the Information Age: Investigating the Roe of the State in Cyberspace* (Aldershot: Ashgate, 2007)

Eatwell, Roger, and Goodwin, Matthew, *National Populism: The Revolt Against Liberal Democracy* (London: Pelican Books, 2018)

Even, Shmuel, and Siman-Tov, David, *Cyber Warfare: Concepts and Strategic Trends* (Tel Aviv: The Institute for National Security Studies, 2012)

Ferguson, Niall, *Colossus: The Rise and Fall of the American Empire* (New York: Penguin Books, 2009)

French, Howard W., *Everything Under the Heavens: How the Past Helps Shapes Chinas Push for Global Power* (New York: Alfred A. Knopf, 2017)

Fukuyama, Francis, *The End of History and the Last Man* (New York: The Free Press, 1992)

Geers, Kenneth (ed.), *Cyber War in Perspective: Russian Aggression Against Ukraine* (Tallinn: NATO CCDCOE, 2015)

Gray, Colin S., *Perspectives on Strategy* (Oxford: Oxford University Press, 2013)

Gray, Colin S., *Theory of Strategy* (Oxford: Oxford University Press, 2018)

Green, James Andrew (ed.), *Cyber Warfare: A Multidisciplinary Analysis* (Abingdon: Routledge, 2015)

Hall Jamieson, Kathleen, *Cyber-War: How Russian Hackers and Trolls Helped Elect a President, What We Don't, Can't, and Do Know* (New York: Oxford University Press, 2018)

Hanson, Fergus, *Internet Wars: The Struggle for Power in the Twenty-First Century* (Haberfield, NSW: Longueville Media, 2015)

Harding, Luke, *The Snowden Files: The Inside Story of the World's Most Wanted Man* (London: Vintage Books, 2014)

Hayden, Michael V., *The Assault on Intelligence: American National Security in an Age of Lies* (New York: Penguin Books, 2018)

Homburger, Zine, Adamson, Liisi, and de Busser, Els (eds.), *Voluntary, Non-Binding Norms for Responsible State Behaviour in the Use of Information and Telecommunications Technology: A Commentary* (2017). Available at www.un.org/disarmament/publications/civilsociety/civil-society-and-disarmament-2017/

Inkster, Nigel, *China's Cyber Power* (London: IISS, 2016)

Isaacson, Walter, *The Innovators: How a Group of Inventors, Hackers, Geniuses, and Geeks Created the Digital Revolution* (London: Simon & Schuster, 2014)

Kagan, Robert, *The World America Made* (New York: Alfred A. Knopf, 2012)

Kakutani, Michiko, *The Death of Truth: Notes on Falsehood in the Age of Trump* (New York: Tim Duggan Books, 2018)

Kello, Lucas, *The Virtual Weapon and International Order* (London: Yale University Press, 2017)

Kennedy, Paul, *The Rise and Fall of the Great Powers: Economic Change and Military Conflict from 1500 to 2000* (New York: Vintage Books, 1987)

Khanna, Parag, *Connectography: Mapping the Future of Global Civilisation* (New York: Random House, 2016)

Kissinger, Henry, *World Order: Reflections on the Characters of Nations and the Course of History* (London: Penguin Books, 2015)

Klimburg, Alexander, *The Darkening Web: The War for Cyberspace* (New York: Penguin Books, 2017)

Krepinevich, Andrew, *7 Deadly Scenarios: A Military Futurist Explores War in the 21st Century* (New York: Bantam Books, 2009)

Leffler, Melvyn P., and Westad, Odd Arne (ed.), *The Cambridge History of the Cold War Vol. I-III* (Cambridge: Cambridge University Press, 2010)

Levitsky, Steven, and Ziblatt, Daniel, *How Democracies Die* (New York: Crown Publishers, 2018)

Lindsay, Jon R., Cheung, Tai Ming, and Reveron, Derek S. (ed.), *China and Cybersecurity: Espionage, Strategy and Politics in the Digital Domain* (New York: Oxford University Press, 2015)

Lucas, Edward, *Cyberphobia: Identity, Trust, Security and the Internet* (London: Bloomsbury, 2016)

Martin Moore, *Democracy Hacked: Political Turmoil and Information Warfare in the Digital Age* (London: Oneworld Publications Ltd., 2018)

Mearshimer, John J., *The Great Delusion: Liberal Dreams and International Realities* (New Haven: Yale University Press, 2018)

Mill, John Stuart, *Littell's Living Ages (Inaugural Address at University of St. Andrews: 01/02/1867) Number 1189, Fourth Series* (Boston, MA: Littell and Gay, 1867)

Mounk, Yascha, *The People vs. Democracy: Why Our Freedom Is in Danger and How to Save It* (Cambridge, MA: Harvard University Press, 2018)

Murray, W. E., *Geographies of Globalisation* (Abingdon: Routledge, 2006)

O'Neill, Cathy, *Weapons of Math Destruction: How Big Data Increases Inequality and Threatens Democracy* (London: Penguin Books, 2017)

Ostrovsky, Arkady, *The Invention of Russia: The Rise of Putin and the Age of Fake News* (New York: Penguin Books, 2017)

Patrikarakos, David, *War in 140 Characters: How Social Media Is Reshaping Conflict in the Twenty-First Century* (New York: Basic Books, 2017)

Pillsbury, Michael, *The Hundred Year Marathon: China's Secret Strategy to Replace America as the Global Superpower* (New York: Henry Holt and Company, 2014)

Powers, Shawn M., and Jablonski, Michael, *The Real Cyber War: The Political Economy of Internet Freedom* (Chicago, IL: University of Illinois Press, 2015)

Rid, Thomas, *Cyber War Will Not Take Place* (London: Hurst & Company, 2013)

Rid, Thomas, *The Rise of the Machines: The Lost History of Cybernetics* (London: Scribe Publications, 2016)

Rosenzweig, Paul, *Cyber Warfare: How Conflicts in Cyberspace Are Challenging America and Changing the World* (Santa Barbara, CA: Praeger, 2013)

Rousseau, Jean-Jacques, *A Treatise on the Social Compact: Or the Principles of Politic Law* (Oxford: Oxford University Press, 1764)

Runciman, David, *How Democracy Ends* (London: Profile Books Ltd, 2018)

Schmitt, Michael N. (ed.), *Tallinn Manual on the International Law Applicable to Cyber Warfare* (Cambridge: Cambridge University Press, 2013)

Schmitt, Michael N. (ed.), *Tallinn Manual 2.0 on the International Law Applicable to Cyber Operations* (Cambridge: Cambridge University Press, 2017)

Schneier, Bruce, *Data and Goliath: The Hidden Battles to Collect Your Data and Control Your World* (New York: W.W. Norton, 2015)

Segal, Adam, *The Hacked World Order: How Nations Fight, Trade, Manoeuvre and Manipulate in the Digital Age* (New York: Public Affairs, 2016)

Shakarian, Paulo, Shakarian, Jana, and Ruef, Andrew, *Introduction to Cyber-Warfare: A Multidisciplinary Approach* (Waltham, MA: Syngress, 2013)

Singer, P. W., and Friedman, Allan, *Cybersecurity and Cyberwar: What Everyone Needs to Know* (New York: Oxford University Press, 2014)

Snyder, Timothy, *On Tyranny: Twenty Lessons from the Twentieth Century* (New York: Tim Duggan Books, 2017)

Snyder, Timothy, *The Road to Unfreedom: Russia, Europe, America* (New York: Tim Duggan Books, 2018)

Steil, Benn, *The Marshall Plan: Dawn of the Cold War* (London: Simon & Schuster, 2018)

Thierer, Adam, and Crews Jr., Clyde Wayne, *Who Rules the Net? Internet Governance and Jurisdiction* (Washington, DC: The Cato Institute, 2003)

Tkacheva, Olesya, Schwartz, Lowell H., Libicki, Martin C., Taylor, Julie E., Martini, Jeffrey, and Baxter, Caroline, *Internet Freedom and Political Space* (Santa Monica, CA: RAND, 2013)

Tooze, Adam, *Crashed: How a Decade of Financial Crises Changed the World* (London: Allan Lane, 2018)

Treisman, Daniel (ed.), *The New Autocracy: Information, Politics, and Policy in Putin's Russia* (Washington, DC: The Brookings Institution, 2018)

Urban, Mark, *The Skripal Files: The Life and Near Death of a Russian Spy* (London: Henry Holt and Company, 2018)

Westwell, Ian, *Condor Legion: The Wehrmacht's Training Ground* (London: Ian Allan Publishing, 2004)

Wittes, Benjamin, and Blum, Gabriella, *The Future of Violence: Robots and Germs, Hackers and Drones* (New York: Basic Books, 2015)

Zetter, Kim, *Countdown to Zero Day: Stuxnet and the Launch of the World's First Digital Weapon* (New York: Crown Publishers, 2014)

Book chapters

Arquilla, John, and Ronfeldt, David, "Cyberwar Is Coming!" in John Arquilla and David Ronfeldt (eds.), *In Athena's Camp: Preparing for Conflict in the Information Age* (Santa Monica, CA: RAND, 1997)

Buzan, Barry, "Economic Structure and International Security: The Limits of the Liberal Case", in Barry Buzan and Lene Hansen (eds.), *International Security Volume II: The Transition to the Post-Cold War Security Agenda* (Los Angeles, CA: Sage Publications Ltd., 2007)

Cerf, Vinton G., 'Foreword: Who Rules the Net?' in Adam Thierer and Clyde Wayne Crews Jr. (eds.), *Who Rules the Net? Internet Governance and Jurisdiction* (Washington, DC: The Cato Institute, 2003)

Crews Jr., Clyde Wayne, And Thierer, Adam, "Introduction: Who Rules the Net?" in Adam Thierer and Clyde Wayne Crews Jr. (eds.), *Who Rules the Net? Internet Governance and Jurisdiction* (Washington, DC: The Cato Institute, 2003)

Dunn Cavelty, Myriam, and Brunner, Elgin M., "Introduction: Information, Power, and Security – An Outline of Debates and Implications", in Myriam Dunn Cavelty, Victor Mauer and Sani Felicia Krishna-Hensel (eds.), *Power and Security in the Information Age: Investigating the Roe of the State in Cyberspace* (Aldershot: Ashgate, 2007)

Ikenberry, G. John, "The Restructuring of the International System After the Cold War", in Melvyn P. Leffler and Odd Arne Westad (eds.), *The Cambridge History of the Cold War Volume III: Endings* (Cambridge: Cambridge University Press, 2010)

Lindsay, Jon R., "Introduction – China and Cybersecurity: Controversy and Context", in Jon R. Lindsay, Tai Ming Cheung and Derek S. Reveron (eds.), *China and Cybersecurity: Espionage, Strategy and Politics in the Digital Domain* (New York: Oxford University Press, 2015)

Steed, Danny, "The Strategic Implications of Cyber Warfare", in James Andrew Green (ed.), *Cyber Warfare: A Multidisciplinary Analysis* (Abingdon: Routledge, 2015)

Tikk, Eneken, "Introduction", in Zine Homburger, Liisi Adamson and Els de Busser (eds.), *Voluntary, Non-Binding Norms for Responsible State Behaviour in the Use of Information and Telecommunications Technology: A Commentary* (2017). Available at www.un.org/disarmament/publications/civilsociety/civil-society-and-disarmament-2017/

Wirtz, James J., "Cyber War and Strategic Culture: The Russian Integration of Cyber Power into Grand Strategy", in Kenneth Geers (ed.), *Cyber War in Perspective: Russian Aggression Against Ukraine* (Tallinn: NATO CCDCOE, 2015)

Industry reports

Baranowski, Sarah, *How Secure Are Root DNS Servers?* (Sans Institute, 2003), p. 1. Available at www.sans.org/reading-room/whitepapers/dns/security-issues-dns-1069 www.sans.org/reading-room/whitepapers/dns/security-issues-dns-1069

Carter, L., Burnett, D., Drew, S., Male, G., Hagadorn, L., Bartlett-McNeil, D., and Irvine, N., *Submarine Cables and the Oceans: Connecting the World* (2009) UNEP-WCMC Biodiversity Series No. 31

Hewlett Packard, *Cyber Risk Report* (various publications). Available at https://ssl.www8.hp.com/ww/en/secure/pdf/4aa6-3786enw.pdf

Hewlett Packard, *State of Security Operations* (2017). Available at https://news.hpe.com/state-of-security-operations-2017/

Infoblox, *Whitepaper: Top Five DNS Security Attack Risks and How to Avoid Them*. Available at www.deepdivenetworking.com/files/infoblox-whitepaper-top5-dns-security-attack-risks-how-to-avoid-them_0.pdf

Kaspersky KSN Report, *Ransomware in 2014–2016* (June 2016). Available at https://securelist.com/pc-ransomware-in-2014-2016/75145/

McAfee, *Economic Impact of Cybercrime – No Slowing Down* (February 2018). Available at www.mcafee.com/enterprise/en-us/solutions/lp/economics-cybercrime.html

Microsoft, *Security Intelligence Report* (various publications). Available at www.microsoft.com/en-gb/security/intelligence-report

Moore, Sara, "Russia Country Profile", *Anomali Intelligence* (August 2017). Available at https://dsimg.ubm-us.net/envelope/393193/563233/Russia%20Country%20Profile.pdf

NTT, *Global Threat Intelligence Report* (2018). Available at www.nttsecurity.com/en-uk/landing-pages/2018-gtir

Scott, James, and Spaniel, Drew, *Rise of the Machines: The Dyn Attack Was Just a Practice Run* (December 2016), Institute for Critical Infrastructure Technology. Available at https://icitech.org/icit-publication-the-rise-of-the-machines-the-dyn-attack-was-just-a-practice-run/

Sungard Availability Services, *Workplace Recovery Case Study: Northgate Information Solutions* (2014). Available at www.sungardas.com/globalassets/_multimedia/document-file/sungardas-northgate-information-solutions-case-study.pdf

Symantec, *Internet Security Threat Report* (various publications). Available at www.symantec.com/security-center/threat-report

Winder, Davey, "How Organised Is Organised Cybercrime?" *Raconteur. Special Report: Cyber-Risk & Resilience* (17 December 2017). Available at www.raconteur.net/risk-management/how-organised-is-organised-cybercrime

Official publications/speeches

China

National Cyberspace Security Strategy (27 December 2016). Available at https://chinacopyrightandmedia.wordpress.com/2016/12/27/national-cyberspace-security-strategy/

Planning Outline for the Construction of a Social Credit System (2014–2020). Posted on 14 June 2014 updated on 25 April 2015, State Council Notice concerning Issuance of the Planning Outline for the Construction of a Social Credit System

(2014–2020) GF No. (2014), p. 21. Available at https://chinacopyrightandmedia. wordpress.com/2014/06/14/planning-outline-for-the-construction-of-a-social-credit-system-2014-2020/

Remarks by H.E. Xi Jinping President of the People's Republic of China at the Opening Ceremony of the Second World Internet Conference (16 December 2015). Available at www.fmprc.gov.cn/mfa_eng/wjdt_665385/zyjh_665391/t1327570. shtml

Israel

Statement to the General Assembly by Foreign Minister Meir (1 March 1957). Available at www.mfa.gov.il/mfa/foreignpolicy/mfadocuments/yearbook1/pages/ 26%20statement%20to%20the%20general%20assembly%20by%20foreign %20mi.aspx

NATO

NATO CCDCOE, *Resources: Cyber Definitions*. Available at https://ccdcoe.org/ cyber-definitions.html

Russia

The Federal Service for the Supervision of Communications, Information Technology, *LinkedIn Refused to Eliminate Violations of Russian Law* (7 March 2017). Available at https://rkn.gov.ru/news/rsoc/news43486.htm

The Ministry of Foreign Affairs of the Russian Federation, *Convention on International Information Security* (22 October 2011). Available at www.mid.ru/ en/foreign_policy/official_documents/-/asset_publisher/CptICkB6BZ29/content/ id/191666

State System of Legal Information, Decree of the President of the Russian Federation No. 646, "On Approving the Doctrine of Information Security for the Russian Federation" (5 December 2016). Available at http://publication.pravo.gov. ru/Document/View/0001201612060002

UK

British Foreign Secretary William Hague, *Security and Freedom in the Cyber Age – Finding the Rules of the Road* (4 February 2011). Available at www.gov. uk/government/speeches/security-and-freedom-in-the-cyber-age-seeking-the-rules-of-the-road

DCMS, *Cyber Security Breaches Survey* (2018). Available at www.gov.uk/govern ment/statistics/cyber-security-breaches-survey-2018

HMG, *The UK Cyber Security Strategy: Protecting and Promoting the UK in a Digital World* (2011). Available at www.gov.uk/government/publications/cyber-security-strategy

Ian Levy, *Active Cyber Defence – One Year on* (2018). Available at www.ncsc.gov.
uk/information/active-cyber-defence-one-year

MoD, *Cyber Primer: Second Edition* (Swindon: DCDC, 2016)

NCSC, *ZTE: NCSC Advice to Select Telecommunications Operators with National
Security Concerns* (16 April 2018). Available at www.ncsc.gov.uk/news/zte-
ncsc-advice-select-telecommunications-operators-national-security-con
cerns-0

Prime Minister Theresa Mays speech to the Lord Mayor's Banquet (13 November 2017). Available at www.gov.uk/government/speeches/pm-speech-to-the-lord-
mayors-banquet-2017

Sir Robert Owen (Chair), *The Litvinenko Inquiry* (2016). Available at www.gov.uk/
government/publications/the-litvinenko-inquiry-report-into-the-death-of-
alexander-litvinenko

Tibbs, Harden, *The Global Cyber Game: The Defence Academy Cyber Inquiry Report*
(London: MoD, 2013)

US

Commission on Enhancing National Cybersecurity, *Report on Securing and
Growing the Digital Economy* (1 December 2016), p. 3. Available at www.nist.
gov/sites/default/files/documents/2016/12/02/cybersecurity-commission-report-
final-post.pdf

Committee on Oversight and Government Reform, US House of Representatives,
114th Congress, *The OPM Data Breach: How the Government Jeopardized Our
National Security for More Than a Generation* (7 October 2016). Available at
https://oversight.house.gov/wp-content/uploads/2016/09/The-OPM-Data-Breach-
How-the-Government-Jeopardized-Our-National-Security-for-More-than-a-Gene
ration.pdf

Executive Office of the President of the United States, *International Strategy for
Cyberspace: Prosperity, Security, and Openness in a Networked World* (2011).
Available at https://obamawhitehouse.archives.gov/sites/default/files/rss_viewer/
internationalstrategy_cyberspace.pdf

FCC, *Restoring Internet Freedom Order* (11 June 2018). Available at https://docs.
fcc.gov/public/attachments/DOC-351481A1.pdf

Grigsby, Alex, "The Year in Review: The Death of the UN GGE Process?" *Council on Foreign Relations* (21 December 2017). Available at www.cfr.org/blog/
year-review-death-un-gge-process

ICS-CERT, Alert (IR-Alert-H-16–056–01), *Cyber-Attack Against Ukrainian Critical
Infrastructure* (25 February 2016). Available at https://ics-cert.us-cert.gov/alerts/
IR-ALERT-H-16-056-01

Kennan, George, *The Charge in the Soviet Union (Kennan) to the Secretary of State*
(22 February 1949), commonly known as "Kennan's Long Telegram" (italics
added). Available at https://nsarchive2.gwu.edu//coldwar/documents/episode-1/
kennan.htm

Masters, Jonathan, "What Is Internet Governance?" *Council on Foreign Relations* (23
April 2014). Available at www.cfr.org/backgrounder/what-internet-governance

National Security Council, *NSC-68: United States Objectives and Programs for National Security* (14 April 1950), p. 64. Available at www.trumanlibrary.org/whistlestop/study_collections/coldwar/documents/pdf/10-1.pdf

Office of the Director of National Intelligence, *Intelligence Community Assessment: Assessing Russian Activities and Intentions in Recent US Elections* (6 January 2017), p. 2. Available at www.dni.gov/files/documents/ICA_2017_01.pdf

Remarks by the President at the Cybersecurity and Consumer Protection Summit (13 February 2015). Available at https://obamawhitehouse.archives.gov/the-press-office/2015/02/13/remarks-president-cybersecurity-and-consumer-protection-summit

Remarks by President Obama and President Xi of the People's Republic of China in a Joint Press Conference (25 October 2015). Available at https://obamawhitehouse.archives.gov/the-press-office/2015/09/25/remarks-president-obama-and-president-xi-peoples-republic-china-joint

Rid, Thomas, "Disinformation: A Primer in Russian Active Measures and Influence Campaigns", Testimony to the 150th Congress (30 March 2017), Hearings before the Select Committee on Intelligence, Unites States Senate. Available at www.intelligence.senate.gov/sites/default/files/documents/os-trid-033017.pdf

The White House, *Remarks by President Obama and Prime Minister Cameron of the United Kingdom in Joint Press Conference* (16 January 2015). Available at https://obamawhitehouse.archives.gov/the-press-office/2015/01/16/remarks-president-obama-and-prime-minister-cameron-united-kingdom-joint-

The US Constitution and Other Key American Writings (San Diego, CA: Word Cloud Classics, 2015)

Statutes

Russia

The Federal Service for the Supervision of Communications, Information Technology, and Mass Media, Federal Law No. 242-FZ. Available at https://pd.rkn.gov.ru/authority/p146/p191/

UK

HMG, *Investigatory Powers Act 2016*. Available at www.legislation.gov.uk/ukpga/2016/25/contents/enacted

Think Tank Reports

Denardis, Laura, *One Internet: An Evidentiary Basis for Policy Making on Internet Universality and Fragmentation* (July 2016), Global Commission on Internet Governance, Paper Series No. 38.

Dewey, Taylor, Kaden, Julianne, Marks, Miriam, Matsushima, Shun, and Zhu, Beijing, *The Impact of Social Media on Social Unrest in the Arab Spring* (2012),

p. viii. Available at https://publicpolicy.stanford.edu/publications/impact-social-media-social-unrest-arab-spring

Drake, William J., Cerf, Vinton G., and Kleinwachter, Wolfgang, *Internet Fragmentation: An Overview* (2016) World Economic Forum, Future of the Internet Initiative White Paper. Available at www.weforum.org/reports/internet-fragmentation-an-overview

Eronen, Pasi, "Russian Hybrid Warfare: How to Confront a New Challenge to the West", *Foundation for Defence of Democracies* (June 2016). Available at www.fdd.org/analysis/2016/06/01/russian-hybrid-warfare-how-to-confront-a-new-challenge-to-the-west/

Freund, Eleanor, *Freedom of Navigation in the South China Sea: A Practical Guide* (June 2017). Available at www.belfercenter.org/publication/freedom-navigation-south-china-sea-practical-guide

Fried, Daniel, and Polyakova, Alina, "Democratic Defense Against Disinformation", *The Atlantic Council* (February 2018). Available at www.atlanticcouncil.org/publications/reports/democratic-defense-against-disinformation

Giles, Keir, *Russia's "New" Tools for Confronting the West: Continuity and Innovation in Moscow's Exercise of Power* (London: Chatham House, March 2016). Available at www.chathamhouse.org/publication/russias-new-tools-confronting-west#

Howard, Philip N., Duffy, Alden, Freelon, Deen, Hussain, Muzammil, Mari, Will, and Muzaid, Marwa, *Opening Closed Regimes: What Was the Role of Social Media During the Arab Spring?* (January 2011) Project on Information Technology and Political Islam, Working Paper

Nagelhus Schia, Niels, and Gjesvik, Lars, *China's Cyber Sovereignty*, Norwegian Institute of International Affairs, Policy Brief (February 2017)

Polyakova, Alina, and Boyer, Spencer P., *The Future of Political Warfare: Russia, the West, and the Coming Age of Global Digital Competition* (March 2018), The Brookings Institute, p. 18. Available at www.brookings.edu/research/the-future-of-political-warfare-russia-the-west-and-the-coming-age-of-global-digital-competition/

Sunak, Rishi, *Undersea Cables: Indispensable, Insecure* (London: Policy Exchange, 2017)

Wheeler, Tom. *Keeping the Internet Open for the Future*, Brookings Institution (20 June 2017). Available at www.brookings.edu/blog/techtank/2017/06/20/keeping-the-internet-open-for-the-future/

Web pages

Ahmed, Murad, Kuchler, Hannah, and Garrahan, Matthew, "How Digital Footprints Paved Way to Weaponising Social Media", *The Financial Times* (18 March 2018). Available at www.ft.com/content/f369e670-2ac3-11e8-9b4b-bc4b9f08f381

Associated Press Security, "Servers Bounce Back from E-Attack", *Wired* (22 October 2002). Available at www.wired.com/2002/10/servers-bounce-back-from-e-attack/

AWS Government, Education & Nonprofits Blog, *Announcing the New AWS Secret Region* (20 November 2017). Available at https://aws.amazon.com/blogs/publicsector/announcing-the-new-aws-secret-region/

Barlow, John Perry, *A Declaration on the Independence of Cyberspace* (8 February 1996). Available at www.eff.org/cyberspace-independence

BBC News, "Russian Spy: What Happened to Sergei and Yulia Skripal?" (27 September 2018). Available at www.bbc.com/news/uk-43643025

BBC News, "MPs Fury Over Mark Zuckerberg 'no show'" (27 November 2018). Available at www.bbc.com/news/technology-46357359

Bloomberg News, "China Tells Carriers to Block Access to Personal VPNs by February" (10 July 2018). Available at www.bloomberg.com/news/articles/2017-07-10/china-is-said-to-order-carriers-to-bar-personal-vpns-by-february

Botsman, Rachel, "Big Data Meets Big Brother as China Moves to Rate Its Citizens", *Wired* (21 October 2017). Available at https:www.wired.co.uk/article/chinese-government-social-credit-score-privacy-invasion

Bowcott, Owen, "Dispute Along Cold War Lines Leads to Collapse of UN Cyberwarfare Talks", *The Guardian* (23 August 2017). Available at www.theguardian.com/world/2017/aug/23/un-cyberwarfare-negotiations-collapsed-in-june-it-emerges

Bowman, Courtney, "Data Localisation Laws: An Emerging Global Trend", *Jurist* (6 January 2017). Available at www.jurist.org/commentary/2017/01/courtney-bowman-data-localization/

Brogan, Jacob, "What Is Internet Governance?" *Slate* (1 November 2016). Available at www.slate.com/articles/technology/future_tense/2016/11/what_exactly_is_internet_governance.html

Brumaghin, Edmund, Gibb, Ross, Mercer, Warren, Molyett, Matthew, and Williams, Craig, "CCleanup: A Vast Number of Machines at Risk", *Cisco Talos* (18 September 2017). Available at https://blog.talosintelligence.com/2017/09/avast-distributes-malware.html

Business Insider, "Vietnam Cyber Law Will Guard Against Fake News, Terrorism – Security Ministry", *Reuters* (31 October 2018). Available at https://uk.reuters.com/article/uk-vietnam-socialmedia/vietnam-cyber-law-will-guard-against-fake-news-terrorism-security-ministry-idUKKCN1N512C

Castillo, Mariano, and Isaac, Lindsay, "Sweden Confirms Foreign Sub in Its Waters", *CNN International* (14 November 2014). Available at https://edition.cnn.com/2014/11/14/world/europe/sweden-russia-submarine-mystery/index.html

CNN, "An Interview with Retired KGB Maj. Gen. Oleg Kalugin" (January 1998). Available at https://web.archive.org/web/20070206020316/www.cnn.com/SPECIALS/cold.war/episodes/21/interviews/kalugin/

CNN Library, "2016 Presidential Election Hacking Fast Facts" (18 October 2018). Available at https://edition.cnn.com/2016/12/26/us/2016-presidential-campaign-hacking-fast-facts/index.html

Computer World, "Complete Transcript, Video of Apple's CEO Tim Cook's EU Privacy Speech" (24 October 2018). Available at www.computerworld.com/article/3315623/security/complete-transcript-video-of-apple-ceo-tim-cooks-eu-privacy-speech.html

Davies, Kim, *There Are Not 13 Root Servers* (13 November 2007). Available at www.icann.org/news/blog/there-are-not-13-root-servers

DHI News Team, "Hemel Explosion Hits Northgate Hospital Customers" (14 December 2005). Available at www.digitalhealth.net/2005/12/hemel-explosion-hits-northgate-hospital-customers/

Elgin, Ben, Lawrence, Dune, and Riley, Michael, "Coke Gets Hacked and Doesn't Tell Anyone", *Bloomberg* (4 November 2012). Available at www.bloomberg. com/news/articles/2012-11-04/coke-hacked-and-doesn-t-tell

Engel, Pamela, "Obama Reportedly Declined to Enforce Red Line in Syria After Iran Threatened to Back Out of Nuclear Deal", *Business Insider* (23 August 2016). Available at http://uk.businessinsider.com/obama-red-line-syria-iran-2016-8? r=US&IR=T

Financial Times, "India's Misguided Move Towards Data Localisation" (10 September 2018). Available at www.ft.com/content/92bb34a8-b4e5-11e8-bbc3-ccd7 de085ffe

Frenkel, Sheer, Confessore, Nicholas, Kang, Cecilia, Rosenberg, Matthew, and Nicas, Jack, "Delay, Deny and Deflect: How Facebook's Leaders Fought Through Crisis", *The New York Times* (14 November 2018). Available at www.nytimes. com/2018/11/14/technology/facebook-data-russia-election-racism.html

Goodwin, Bill, "As Firms Count Cost of Oil Depot Blast, What Are the Disaster Recovery Lessons?" *Computer Weekly Blog* (January 2006). Available at www. computerweekly.com/feature/As-firms-count-cost-of-oil-depot-blast-what-are-the-disaster-recovery-lessons

Gorman, Siobhan, "Electricity Grid in the US Penetrated by Spies", *The Wall Street Journal* (8 April 2009). Available at www.wsj.com/articles/SB12391480 5204099085

Gorman, Siobhan, "China Hackers Hit US Chamber", *The Wall Street Journal* (21 December 2011). Available at www.wsj.com/articles/SB10001424052970 204058404577110541568535300

Greenberg, Andy, "Hacker Lexicon: What Is DNS Hijacking?" *Wired* (9 April 2017). Available at www.wired.com/story/what-is-dns-hijacking/

Greenberg, Andy, "How an Entire Nation Became Russia's Test Lab for Cyberwar", *Wired* (20 June 2017). Available at www.wired.com/story/russian-hackers-attack-ukraine/

Greenberg, Andy, "China Tests the Limits of Its US Hacking Truce", *Wired* (31 October 2017). Available at www.wired.com/story/china-tests-limits-of-us-hacking-truce/

Greenberg, Andy, "The Untold Story of NotPetya, the Most Devastating Cyberattack in History", *Wired* (22 August 2018). Available at www.wired. com/story/notpetya-cyberattack-ukraine-russia-code-crashed-the-world/

Harding, Luke, "The Node Pole: Inside Facebook's Swedish Hub Near the Arctic Circle", *The Guardian* (25 September 2015). Available at www.theguardian. com/technology/2015/sep/25/facebook-datacentre-lulea-sweden-node-pole

Harold, Scott W., "The US-China Cyber Agreement: A Good First Step", *The RAND Blog* (1 August 2016). Available at www.rand.org/blog/2016/08/the-us-china-cyber-agreement-a-good-first-step.html

Has, Benjamin, "China Moves to Block VPNs from 2018", *The Guardian* (11 July 2017). Available at www.theguardian.com/world/2017/jul/11/china-moves-to-block-internet-vpns-from-2018

Howell, Catherine, and West, Darrell M., *The Internet as a Human Right*, Brookings Institution (7 November 2016). Available at www.brookings.edu/blog/tech tank/2016/11/07/the-internet-as-a-human-right/

ICANN, *Factsheet: Root Server Attack on 6 February 2007* (1 March 2007). Available at www.icann.org/en/system/files/files/factsheet-dns-attack-08mar07-en.pdf

ICANN, *How Does ICANN Work?* Available at www.icann.org/resources/pages/welcome-2012-02-25-en

ICANN, *What Does ICANN Do?* Available at www.icann.org/resources/pages/welcome-2012-02-25-en

ICANN, *General ICANN Factsheet* (November 2013). Available at www.icann.org/resources/pages/factsheets-2012-02-25-en

ICANN, *The IANA Functions* (December 2015). Available at www.icann.org/en/system/files/files/iana-functions-18dec15-en.pdf

Idrisova, Ksenia, "Explainer: What Is Russia's New VPN Law All About", *BBC Monitoring* (1 November 2017). Available at www.bbc.com/news/technology-41829726

Information Age, "Getting Back to Business After Buncefield", (16 April 2006). Available at www.information-age.com/getting-back-to-business-after-buncefield-284331/

The Internet Society, *Brief History of the Internet* (1997). Available at www.internetsociety.org/internet/history-internet/brief-history-internet/

The Internet Society, *Our Mission*. Available at www.internetsociety.org/mission/

Kaplan, Fred, "The Info Wars to Come", *Slate* (8 September 2017). Available at https://slate.com/news-and-politics/2017/09/russia-is-weaponizing-social-media.html

Kendrick, Katherine, "Data Localisation: Risky Business", *Forbes* (19 February 2015). Available at www.forbes.com/sites/realspin/2015/02/19/risky-business-data-localization/#474573751077

Kesari, Vinay, "Data Localisation and the Danger of a 'splinternet'", *Factor Daily* (26 July 2018). Available at https://factordaily.com/data-localisation-and-the-danger-of-splinternet/

Lunden, Ingrid, "Russia Says '*nyet*', Continues LinkedIn Block After It Refuses to Store Data in Russia", *TechCrunch* (7 March 2017). Available at https://techcrunch.com/2017/03/07/russia-says-nyet-continues-linkedin-block-after-it-refuses-to-store-data-in-russia/

MacAskill, Ewen, "Major Cyber-Attack on UK a Matter of 'when, not if' – Security Chief", *The Guardian* (23 January 2018). Available at www.theguardian.com/technology/2018/jan/22/cyber-attack-on-uk-matter-of-when-not-if-says-security-chief-ciaran-martin

MacAskill, Ewan, Border, Julian, Hopkins, Nick, Davies, Nick, and Ball, James, "GCHQ Taps Fibre-Optics Cables for Secret Access to World's Communications", *The Guardian* (21 June 2013). Available at www.theguardian.com/uk/2013/jun/21/gchq-cables-secret-world-communications-nsa

Marcus, Jonathan, "Russia vs the West: Is This a New Cold War?" *BBC News* (1 April 2018). Available at www.bbc.com/news/world-europe-43581449

Margolin, Jack, "Russia, China, and the Push for 'Digital Sovereignty'" (2 December 2016). Available at https://theglobalobservatory.org/2016/12/russia-china-digital-sovereignty-shanghai-cooperation-organization/

McNamee, Roger, "How to Fix Facebook – Before It Fixes Us", *Washington Monthly* (January–March 2018). Available at https://washingtonmonthly.com/magazine/january-february-march-2018/how-to-fix-facebook-before-it-fixes-us/

Menn, Joseph, and Finkle, Joe, "Chinese Economic Cyber-Espionage Plummets in US: Experts", *Reuters* (21 June 2016). Available at www.reuters.com/article/us-cyber-spying-china/chinese-economic-cyber-espionage-plummets-in-u-s-experts-idUSKCN0Z700D

Metz, Case, "Amazon Wins Victory in Quest for Top Secret CIA Cloud", *Wired* (8 October 2013). Available at www.wired.com/2013/10/amazon-cia-2/

Microsoft, *How TCP/IP Works*. Available at https://technet.microsoft.com/en-gb/library/cc786128(v=ws.10).aspx

Moody, Oliver, "Big Brother Is Watching Them. And We're Next", *The Times* (31 March 2018), p. 33

Mozur, Paul, "Inside China's Dystopian Dreams: A.I., Shame and Lots of Cameras", *The New York Times* (8 July 2018). Available at www.nytimes.com/2018/07/08/business/china-surveillance-technology.html

Nakashima, Ellan, and Sonne, Paul, "China Hacked a Navy Contractor and Secured a Trove of Highly Sensitive Data on Submarine Warfare", *The Washington Post* (8 June 2018). Available at www.washingtonpost.com/world/national-security/china-hacked-a-navy-contractor-and-secured-a-trove-of-highly-sensitive-data-on-submarine-warfare/2018/06/08/6cc396fa-68e6-11e8-bea7-c8eb28bc52b1_story.html?noredirect=on&utm_term=.b579d3932ba1

Newton, Matthew, and Summers, Julia, *Russian Data Localisation Laws: Enriching 'Security' and the Economy* (28 February 2018). Available at https://jsis.washington.edu/news/russian-data-localization-enriching-security-economy/

Oliphant, Roland, and Soulsby, Darren, "Mapped: Just How Many Incursions into NATO Airspace Has Russian Military Made?" *The Telegraph* (15 May 2015). Available at www.telegraph.co.uk/news/worldnews/europe/russia/11609783/Mapped-Just-how-many-incursions-into-Nato-airspace-has-Russian-military-made.html

Oxford English Dictionary Word of the Year 2016. Available at https://en.oxforddictionaries.com/word-of-the-year/word-of-the-year-2016

Parfitt, Tom, "Operation Troy: The Blueprint for Spreading Chaos in Ukraine", *The Times* (2 April 2018), p. 8. Available at www.thetimes.co.uk/article/operation-troy-russia-s-blueprint-for-spreading-chaos-in-ukraine-x2bqv7hbg

Pham, Sherisse, "Use iCloud in China? Prepare to Share Your Data with a State-Run Firm", *CNN Business* (11 January 2018). Available at https://money.cnn.com/2018/01/10/technology/apple-china-icloud/index.html

Pham, Sherisse, "Apple Is Under Fire for Moving iCloud Data to China", *CNN Business* (28 February 2018). Available at https://money.cnn.com/2018/02/28/technology/apple-icloud-data-china/index.html

Ramsey, Carly, and Wootliff, Carl, "China's Cybersecurity Law: The Impossibility of Compliance?" *Forbes* (29 May 2017). Available at www.forbes.com/sites/riskmap/2017/05/29/chinas-cyber-security-law-the-impossibility-of-compliance/#5ba10c53471c

Robertson, Jordan, and Riley, Michael, "The Big Hack: How China Used a Tiny Chip to Infiltrate US Companies", *Bloomberg Businessweek* (4 October 2018). Available at www.bloomberg.com/news/features/2018-10-04/the-big-hack-how-china-used-a-tiny-chip-to-infiltrate-america-s-top-companies

Roettgers, Janko, "Apple Denies Bloomberg's China Hack Report in Letter to Congress", *Variety* (8 October 2018). Available at https://variety.com/2018/digital/news/apple-denies-bloombergs-china-hack-report-in-letter-to-congress-1202972155/

Rogin, Josh, "NSA Chief: Cybercrime Constitute 'the greatest transfer of wealth in history'", *Foreign Policy* (12 July 2012). Available at https://foreignpolicy.com/2012/07/09/nsa-chief-cybercrime-constitutes-the-greatest-transfer-of-wealth-in-history/

Rollet, Charles, "The Odd Reality of Life Under China's All-Seeing Credit Score System", *Wired* (5 June 2018). Available at www.wired.co.uk/article/china-social-credit

Romm, Tony, "Facebook's Zuckerberg Just Survived 10 Hours of Questioning by Congress", *The Washington Post* (11 April 2018). Available at www.washingtonpost.com/news/the-switch/wp/2018/04/11/zuckerberg-facebook-hearing-congress-house-testimony/?utm_term=.3ff93cbec654

Roth, Andrew, and Dodd, Vikram, "Salisbury Poisoning Suspect Identified as Russian Colonel", *The Guardian* (26 September 2018). Available at www.theguardian.com/world/2018/sep/26/salisbury-poisoning-suspect-is-russian-colonel-reports

Sabur, Rozina, and Alexander, Harriet, "US Imposes Sanctions on Russia Over Salisbury Poisoning of Skripals", *The Telegraph* (8 September 2018). Available at www.telegraph.co.uk/news/2018/08/08/us-imposes-sanctions-russia-salisbury-spy-poisoning/

Sanders, Katie, "Did Vladimir Putin Call the Breakup of the USSR 'the greatest geopolitical tragedy of the 20th century'?" *Politifact* (6 March 2014). Available at www.politifact.com/punditfact/statements/2014/mar/06/john-bolton/did-vladimir-putin-call-breakup-ussr-greatest-geop/

Sanger, David E., and Myers, Steven Lee, "After a Hiatus, China Accelerates Cyberspying Efforts to Obtain US Technology", *The New York Times* (29 November 2018). Available at www.nytimes.com/2018/11/29/us/politics/china-trump-cyberespionage.html

Seely, Bob, and Sandra, Alya, "The Toolkit for Kremlin's New Warfare", *The Times* (2 April 2018), p. 9. Available at www.thetimes.co.uk/article/the-toolkit-for-kremlin-s-new-warfare-6kthqgd7t

Servers.global, *Meeting the Challenge of Data Localisation Laws* (30 November 2016). Available at www.servers.global/meeting-the-challenge-of-data-localization-laws/

Sharikov, Pasha, *Understanding the Russian Approach to Information Security* (16 January 2018). Available at www.europeanleadershipnetwork.org/commentary/understanding-the-russian-approach-to-information-security/

Shevchenko, Vitaly, " 'Little green men' or 'Russian invaders'?" *BBC News* (11 March 2014). Available at www.bbc.com/news/world-europe-26532154

Solon, Olivia, "China Cracks Down on VPNs, Making It Harder to Circumvent the Great Firewall", *The Guardian* (23 January 2017). Available at www.theguardian.com/technology/2017/jan/23/china-vpn-cleanup-great-firewall-censorship

Start, Nick, "How an Army of Vulnerable Gadgets Took Down the Internet Today", *The Verge* (21 October 2016). Available at www.theverge.com/2016/10/21/13362354/dyn-dns-ddos-attack-cause-outage-status-explained

Tarnoff, Ben, "How the Internet Was Invented", *The Guardian* (15 July 2016). Available at www.theguardian.com/technology/2016/jul/15/how-the-internet-was-invented-1976-arpa-kahn-cerf

Webb, Tim, "Firms Still Missing Data Lost in Buncefield Oil Depot Blaze", *The Independent* (1 January 2006). Available at www.independent.co.uk/news/business/news/firms-still-missing-data-lost-in-buncefield-oil-depot-blaze-335867.html

Wei, Yuxi, *China-Russia Cybersecurity Cooperation: Working Towards Cyber-Sovereignty* (21 June 2016). Available at https://jsis.washington.edu/news/china-russia-cybersecurity-cooperation-working-towards-cyber-sovereignty/

Williams, Brad D., "How Russia Adapted KGB 'active measures' to Cyber Operations, Part I", *Fifth Domain* (19 March 2017). Available at www.fifthdomain.com/home/2017/03/19/how-russia-adapted-kgb-active-measures-to-cyber-operations-part-i/

Wylie, Christopher, "Why I Broke Facebook Data Story – and What Should Happen Now", *The Observer* (8 April 2018)

Yang, Yuan, "China's Cyber Security Law Rattles Multinationals", *The Financial Times* (30 May 2017). Available at www.ft.com/content/b302269c-44ff-11e7-8519-9f94ee97d996

Zetter, Kim, "Report: Hackers Seized Control of Computers in NASA's Jet Propulsion Lab", *Wired* (3 January 2012). Available at www.wired.com/2012/03/jet-propulsion-lab-hacked/

Index

Note: Page numbers in *italics* indicate figures on the corresponding pages.